KEEP CALM
AND
TAKE ANOTHER
TEA BREAK

By Stephen Francis & Rico

JACANA

For our wives, Bronwyn and Danya,

for putting up with the deadlines, the punchlines and the three other women in our lives

Published in 2013 in South Africa by
Jacana Media
10 Orange Street, Auckland Park, 2092
PO Box 291784, Melville, 2109
www.jacana.co.za

ISBN 978-1-4314-0843-6
Job number 002087
Printed and bound by Ultra Litho (Pty) Ltd, Johannesburg

OTHER MADAM & EVE BOOKS

Madam & Eve Collection (Rapid Phase, 1993, reprint 1999)
Free At Last (Penguin Books, 1994)
All Aboard for the Gravy Train (Penguin Books, 1995)
Somewhere over the Rainbow Nation (Penguin Books, 1996)
Madam & Eve's Greatest Hits (Penguin Books, 1997)
Madams are from Mars, Maids are from Venus (Penguin Books, 1997)
It's a Jungle Out There (David Philip, 1998)
International Maid of Mystery (David Philip, 1999)
Has anyone seen my Vibrating Cellphone? (interactive.Africa, 2000)
The Madams are Restless (Rapid Phase, 2000)
Crouching Madam, Hidden Maid (Rapid Phase, 2001)
Madam & Eve, 10 Wonderful Years (Rapid Phase, 2002)
The Maidtrix (Rapid Phase, 2003)
Gin & Tonic for the Soul (Rapid Phase, 2004)
Desperate Housemaids (Rapid Phase, 2005)
Madams of the Caribbean (Rapid Phase, 2006)
Bring me my (new) Washing Machine (Rapid Phase, 2007)

Madam & Eve Unplugged (Rapid Phase, 2008)
Strike While The Iron Is Hot (Jacana, 2009)
Twilight of the Vuvuzelas (Jacana, 2010)
Mother Anderson's Secret Book of Wit & Wisdom (Jacana, 2011)
The Pothole at the End of the Rainbow (Jacana, 2011)
Twenty (Jacana, 2012)
Jamen sort kaffe er pa mode nu, Madam! (Gyldendal, Denmark, 1995)
Jeg gyver Mandela Skylden for det her! (Gyldendal, Denmark, 1995)
Alt under kontrol I Sydafrika! (Bogfabrikken, Denmark, 1997)
Men alla dricker kaffet svart nufortiden, Madam! (Bokfabrikken, Sweden, 1998)
Madame & Eve, Enfin Libres! (Vents D'Ouest, France, 1997)
Votez Madame & Eve (Vents D'Ouest, France, 1997)
La coupe est pleine (Vents D'Ouest, France, 1998)
Rennue-Ménage à deux (Vents D'Ouest, France, 1999)
En voient de toutes les couleurs (Vents D'Ouest, France, 2000)
Madame vient de Mars, Eve de Venus (Vents D'Ouest, France, 2000)
Madam & Eve (LIKE, Finland, 2005)

MADAM & EVE APPEARS REGULARLY IN:
Mail & Guardian, The Star, Saturday Star, Sunday Times, Herald, Mercury, Witness, Daily Dispatch, Cape Times, Pretoria News, Diamond Fields Advertiser, Die Volksblad, EC Today, Kokstad Advertiser, The Namibian.

TO CONTACT MADAM & EVE:
PO Box 413667, Craighall 2024, Johannesburg, South Africa
ricos@rapidphase.co.za
www.madamandeve.co.za

THE WORLD ACCORDING TO ZUMA

ISLE OF ZUMA
ZUMA LANDFILL
MOUNT ZUMA
ZUMA RIVER
ZUMA VALLEY
ZUMA LAKE
ZUMA ZOO
ZUMA CITY
ZUMA INDUSTRIAL PARK
ZUMALAND
ZUMA FALLS
ZUMA BEACH
CLIFFS OF ZUMA
CAPE ZUMA
ZUMA SWAMP
ZUMA FOREST
ZUMAVILLE
ZUMA BAY

| ZUMAVILLE | BHEKIVILLE | ZILLEVILLE | MARGARITAVILLE |

FOR RENT
TO LET
TO LET
SAPS

I'M WORRIED ABOUT THE **PRESIDENT**. THE COUNTRY'S IN CRISIS AND HE'S LOSING **FOCUS**.

...YOU THINK?

WOO! WOO! ALL ABOARD!!

ZUMAVILLE! ...NEXT STOP ZUMAVILLE!!

CHOOGA! CHOOGA! CHOOGA!

...FIND THE ARCHITECT WHO BUILT THIS AND ARREST HIM.

I'M ON IT.

WOO! WOO! MORE COAL, DAMMIT! MORE COAL!!

MADAM & Eve

BY STEPHEN FRANCIS & RICO

YOU WANTED TO SEE US, MISTER PRESIDENT?

YES! LOOK AT THIS -- THE ARCHITECTS HAVE DONE AN AMAZING JOB!

AND YOU THOUGHT *ZUMAVILLE* WAS GOOD.

"ZUMALAND?"

VERY...UH, IMPRESSIVE, SIR.

"IMPRESSIVE?" IT CAN'T **MISS!** CHECK OUT THESE ATTRACTIONS!

"IT'S A SMALL FIRST CLASS WORLD AFTER ALL!"

OVER HERE ... "MR. TOAD'S WILD BLUE LIGHT ENTOURAGE RIDE."

THIS ONE LOOKS GOOD-- "FINDING NEMO SA NAVY **SUBMARINE** VOYAGE."

FORGET IT. OUT OF ORDER. DOESN'T WORK.

LOOK! "SERVICE DELIVERY MOUNTAIN!"

FORGET IT-- IT'S LOCATED BETWEEN "TOMORROWLAND" AND "FANTASYLAND."

LOOK-- "PETER PAN'S FLIGHT TO AUSTRALIA!"

...AND "EMIGRATION ISLAND."

CUTE-- "SLEEPING BEAUTY'S CASTLE"... THEY'RE ALL **ASLEEP.**

NAH...THAT'S JUST **PARLIAMENT.**

© RAPID PHASE - 2012

...AND I HAVE HIGH HOPES FOR THESE TWO ATTRACTIONS... "TAX PAYER ISLAND"... AND "PINOCCHIO'S PERMANENT JOURNEY TO NEW ZEALAND."

MAYBE YOU SHOULD **LIE DOWN,** SIR.

CAREFUL ... YOU'RE LEANING ON "ZUMA'S WIVES OF THE CARIBBEAN!"

HOW COME THEY **SHOT** ALL THOSE STRIKING MINEWORKERS?

LABOUR DISPUTES ARE COMPLICATED. I GUESS THE POLICE AND MINE MANAGEMENT <u>WON</u>.

WHY DO YOU SAY <u>THAT</u>?

THE MINERS ARE BACK **UNDERGROUND**, AREN'T THEY?

www.madamandeve.co.za

MAYBE THIS WILL ALL MAKE **SENSE** WHEN WE'RE OLDER.

I HOPE NOT.

©RAPID PHASE-2012

CHECK THIS OUT.

A NEW TOY?

YES, IT'S A SPECIAL EDITION RADIO-CONTROLLED SOUTH AFRICAN NAVY SUBMARINE.

HOW DOES IT WORK?

©RAPID PHASE - 2012

IT **DIVES** RIGHT TO THE **BOTTOM** AND THEN **BREAKS DOWN**.

CAN YOU FIX IT?

NOT YET... "DRY DOCK SOLD SEPARATELY."

www.madamandeve.co.za

PSHHHH!

SPRITZ! SPRITZ!

www.madamandeve.co.za

MADAM -- CAN I HAVE A **WAGE** INCREASE?

WHATEVER YOU WANT, OH MOST WONDERFUL MAID IN THE WORLD.

©RAPID PHASE - 2012

HOW'D YOU GET YOUR MADAM TO GIVE YOU A **RAISE?**

OVEN CLEANER, FLOOR WAX AND FURNITURE POLISH.

7

GUESS WHAT? WE'RE STUDYING **APARTHEID** IN SCHOOL ALL THIS MONTH.

GOOD FOR YOU. IT'S **IMPORTANT** YOU PAY ATTENTION.

I KNOW. I JUST HOPE I CAN **UNDERSTAND** ALL OF IT.

WHY?

...I'M NOT THAT GOOD AT BIOLOGY.

THANDI, DIDN'T YOU TELL ME YOU'RE STUDYING **APARTHEID** IN SCHOOL NEXT WEEK?

I'M NOT LOOKING FORWARD TO IT. I **HATE** BIOLOGY.

HERE'S A NEWS FLASH: "APARTHEID" **ISN'T** BIOLOGY!

MATHS? ...SCIENCE?

HISTORY.

EVEN **WORSE!** WE **HATE** HISTORY! **WHEN** WAS IT?

WELL... TECHNICALLY, RIGHT UP UNTIL 1994.

1994?! AUGH! THAT'S **ANCIENT** HISTORY!

WE'RE GOING TO NEED **LOTS** OF CRIB SHEETS.

EVE!! WHERE'S MY **GIN & TONIC?!!**

HAVE YOU STARTED YOUR READING ABOUT "APARTHEID" FOR SCHOOL YET?

OF COURSE.

ACTUALLY, THE APARTHEIDONIANS WERE AN INTERESTING PEOPLE.

"APARTHEIDONIANS?"

THEY SUCCESSFULLY FOUGHT THE **VIKINGS** AND DEVELOPED THE WORLD'S FIRST POSTAL SYSTEM.

LET ME KNOW WHEN YOU **REALLY** START READING ABOUT IT.

EITHER SHE KNOWS HER APARTHEID HISTORY **WELL** ... OR MY **GUESS** WAS **WAY** OFF.

I THOUGHT THE "POSTAL SYSTEM" WAS A NICE TOUCH.

MADAM & Eve

BY STEPHEN FRANCIS & RICO

SIGH.

WHAT ARE YOU DOING SITTING ON THE **STOEP**? I DIDN'T EVEN KICK YOU OUT YET.

I FINALLY STARTED READING ABOUT **APARTHEID** FOR MY SCHOOL **HISTORY** CLASS.

I SEE. ...AND?

AT FIRST I THOUGHT THERE MUST BE SOME **MISTAKE**. MAYBE THIS BOOK WAS PUBLISHED IN **LIMPOPO** AND THEY GOT IT ALL WRONG... THAT IT **COULDN'T** HAVE **HAPPENED** LIKE THEY SAY!

WHY DIDN'T SOMEBODY **DO** SOMETHING?!

MANY **DID**. AT GREAT **SACRIFICE**.

WHAT'S **WRONG** WITH **PEOPLE** ANYWAY?!!!

THEY PUT **MADIBA** IN PRISON! HOW COULD THEY PUT **MADIBA** IN PRISON?!

I DON'T KNOW.

THE IMPORTANT THING IS THAT WE **LEARN** FROM HISTORY--NOT TO MAKE THE **SAME** MISTAKES... AND HONOUR OUR FRAGILE HARD-WON **DEMOCRACY**.

©RAPID PHASE - 2012

AND IN TODAY'S HEADLINES, THE STRIKING MARIKANA WORKERS, SHOT BY POLICE, WERE **BURIED** TODAY... EXPERTS ESTIMATE THAT GRAFT AND CORRUPTION HAS **COST** SOUTH AFRICA R 675 BILLION SINCE 1994...

Panel 1: "AND SO", SAID **RUMPEL-STILTSKIN**... "IF YOU **GUESS** MY NAME, I'LL SPIN STRAW INTO **GOLD** AND MAKE YOU **RICH!**"

Panel 2: WELL, THEY NEVER **DID** GUESS HIS NAME... INSTEAD, THEY GAVE HIM A **NEW** ONE.

MOM!!

Panel 3: ...PLUS A VALID I.D., A DRIVER'S LICENCE, PROOF OF RESIDENCE... AND **BOB** NEVER HAD TO GO BACK TO **HOME AFFAIRS** AGAIN.

Panel 4: WHO'S "**BOB**"?

WHAT? I **UPDATED** IT A LITTLE.

"**RUMPEL-STILTSKIN**." TRY AND KEEP UP.

Panel 5: **LERATO!** LERATO! LERATO! ARE YOU ALL RIGHT?

Panel 6: STRANGE... ONE MOMENT, I WAS LISTENING TO THE **RADIO**... AND THE NEXT THING I KNOW, I **FAINTED.**

THAT **IS** STRANGE.

Panel 7: CONTINUING WITH TODAY'S TOP STORY... PRESIDENT ZUMA SAYS THAT "**SERVICE DELIVERY** IN SOUTH AFRICA IS **EXCEPTIONAL**... AND SOME PEOPLE THINK OTHERWISE DUE TO **UNBALANCED REPORTING**."

Panel 8: CRASH! CRASH! CRASH! CRASH! **CRASH!!** CRASH!

Panel 9: MISTER PRESIDENT, ARE YOU SAYING THAT **SERVICE DELIVERY** IS **EXCELLENT?**

YES! IF IT WEREN'T FOR THE **MEDIA'S** "**UNBALANCED REPORTING**", PEOPLE WOULD SEE THAT!

Panel 10: OUR COUNTRY'S **INFRASTRUCTURE** IS AS **SOLID** AS THIS **PODIUM!**

BONK!!

Panel 11: **CRASH!!**

Panel 12: WELL... HE GOT THAT RIGHT.

EISH.

©RAPID PHASE · 2012

www.madamandeve.co.za

MADAM & Eve

BY STEPHEN FRANCIS & RICO

"HERE COME THE BULLDOZERS."

BRRRRR RRRRR

LIMPOPO

"BUT SOMETHING IS ROTTEN IN LIMPOPO."

HEY! YOU CALL THESE **PAVED ROADS**?! IT'S MOSTLY <u>SAND</u>!!

SEE IF I GIVE **YOU** ANOTHER **ILLEGAL TENDER**!

OKAY, FINE.

HERE'S ANOTHER KICKBACK.

© RAPID PHASE · 2012

YOU THINK I'M A MORON?! THAT IS MONOPOLY MONEY!

IT'S ALL I **HAVE**!

100

THEN TAKE YOUR BULLDOZERS AND GET OUT OF HERE!

OH YEAH? ...THEN SAY HELLO TO MY **LITTLE FRIEND**!

AAHH!! GRRRRR!!

A T-REX IN LIMPOPO?! ...GIVE ME BACK MY LEGO MAN!!

I TOLD YOU I'D GET YOUR STUPID KICKBACK!

CHOMP!

THINGS HAVE CHANGED SINCE I WAS A KID.

THE COMEBACK TRAIL

♪ GETTIN STRONG, NOW! ROCKY'S STRONG NOW! ♪

WHEEZE! PUFF! PUFF! PUFF! WHEEZE! PUFF!

IT'S NO GOOD. **JULIUS** IS WAY TOO OUT OF SHAPE.

WHEEZE! PUFF! PUFF!

JUJU

HE NEEDS A **TRAINER**.

CRASH!

BETTER CALL YOU-KNOW-WHO.

www.madamandeve.co.za ©RAPID PHASE · 2012

ENTER THE DRACONIAN

MASTER THABO, WE NEED YOU.

SHH. I'M MEDITATING.

JULIUS -- THIS IS **MASTER THABO**. HE HAS RELUCTANTLY AGREED TO HELP **TRAIN** YOU FOR YOUR BIG **COMEBACK**.

"MASTER THABO?"

FIRST -- YOU MUST GET BACK THE "**EYE** OF THE TIGER."

WHAT TIGER? THERE AREN'T ANY **TIGERS** IN AFRICA.

WRONG! THE **ALIENS** BRED THEM WHILE RESEARCHING A **CURE** FOR **HIV**! DON'T YOU CRUISE THE **INTERNET**?

©RAPID PHASE · 2012 www.madamandeve.co.za

ARE YOU **SURE** ABOUT THIS GUY?

AND LOSE THE **BERET**.

COMEBACK TRAINING

JULIUS... I AM HERE TO HELP YOU GET BACK THE "**EYE** OF THE TIGER."

BUT **HOW**, MASTER THABO?

IT'S A **ZEN** THING. SEE THIS **SPOON**? THERE **IS NO** SPOON! SEE THIS **FORK**? THERE **IS NO** FORK!

MASTER THABO... HOW WILL "NO SPOON" AND "NO FORK" **HELP** MY POLITICAL COMEBACK?

BY HELPING YOUR **WAISTLINE**. YOU NEED TO LOSE **TEN KILOS**.

©RAPID PHASE · 2012 www.madamandeve.co.za

MASTER THABO -- **LOOK**! THE **ICE CREAM VAN**!

THERE **IS NO** ICE CREAM VAN.

14

Panel 1:
GETTING BACK "THE EYE OF THE TIGER."

REMEMBER, JULIUS...TO LEARN MY TEACHINGS ...I MUST FIRST TEACH YOU TO LEARN.

Panel 2:
BUT... MASTER THABO...

AH-AH! HE WHO QUESTIONS TRAINING...ONLY TRAINS HIMSELF AT ASKING QUESTIONS.

Panel 3:
... HE WHO IS OPEN TO A CHALLENGE ...ALWAYS CHALLENGES HIMSELF TO BE OPEN.

MASTER THABO... SOMETIMES YOU MAKE NO SENSE.

©RAPID PHASE - 2012

Panel 4:
GOOD! YOU'RE LEARNING! IT TOOK THE VOTERS YEARS TO FIGURE THAT OUT.

WHEN'S LUNCH?

Panel 5:
CONGRATULATIONS, JULIUS. I HAVE GIVEN YOU BACK "THE EYE OF THE TIGER."

THANK YOU, MASTER THABO.

Panel 6:
BUT NOW... YOU NEED TO AQUIRE "THE EYE OF THE POLITICIAN."

EISH -- MORE TRAINING?!

www.madamandeve.co.za

Panel 7:
YES... BUT YOU'LL ENJOY THIS... I CALL IT "GRAVY TRAINING."

©RAPID PHASE - 2012

Panel 8:
GONG!

BRING OUT THE SUSHI AND SINGLE MALT WHISKEY!

AT LAST.

Panel 9:
WHEN EVERY MINER STANDS UP AGAINST THE GOVERNMENT FOR ABANDONING YOUR NEEDS... I WILL BE WITH YOU!

YAY!!

CLAP! CLAP! CLAP! CLAP!

www.madamandeve.co.za

Panel 10:
WHEN THE POLICE ARRIVE WITH THEIR RIFLES AND ORDER YOU TO DISPERSE ... I WILL BE WITH YOU!

YAY!!

CLAP! CLAP! CLAP! CLAP!

Panel 11:
... AND WHEN ZUMA CAVES IN, YOU GET YOUR WAGE INCREASE AND IT'S TIME TO GO BACK TO WORK AT THE BOTTOM OF A DEEP, DARK MINE ...

CLAP! CLAP! CLAP!

©RAPID PHASE - 2012

Panel 12:
...FLOYD WILL BE WITH YOU!

HUH? SAY WHAT?

YAY!!

CLAP! CLAP! CLAP! CLAP!

FRIENDS
OF ANYONE BUT ZUMA

SIGN UP HERE

www.madamandeve.co.za

© RAPID PHASE - 2012

AND IN OTHER NEWS, JULIUS MALEMA...

AAAAH!! I'M SO **TIRED** OF **HEARING** ABOUT **MALEMA!**

FROM **NOW** ON, THE NEXT PERSON THAT MENTIONS **MALEMA** HAS TO PAY A **FINE** OF **FIVE RAND!**

FIVE RAND... JUST FOR SAYING **"JULIUS?"**

NO, FOR SAYING **"MALEMA!"**

AHA!! **FIVE RAND!**

SLAM!!

GROWNUPS... THEY MAKE THE RULES... THEN THEY'RE THE **FIRST** TO **BREAK** THEM.

© RAPID PHASE - 2012 www.madamandeve.co.za

MALEMA

This cartoon is a Malema-free zone. There will be no mention of Malema.

I FEEL MUCH BETTER NOW! TO HAVE A **BREAK** FROM THAT TIRED, REPETITIVE REFRAIN. ...SO : WHAT SHALL WE **TALK** ABOUT?

ZUMA?

© RAPID PHASE - 2012

ZUMA

This cartoon is also a Zuma-free zone. There will be no mention of Zuma.

16

MADAM & Eve

BY STEPHEN FRANCIS & RICO

AND IN OTHER NEWS... INVESTIGATIONS SHOW THAT THE **R 238 MILLION** SPENT ON **NKANDLA** MAY JUST BE THE **TIP OF THE ICEBERG**...

...AN ADDITIONAL **R 528 MILLION** OF TAXPAYERS' MONEY WAS SPENT ON THE **ROAD** LEADING THERE.

AAAAH!!

YOU WANTED TO SEE ME, SIR?

YES.

DID YOU READ TODAY'S **PAPERS**?

NOT YET, SIR.

"NKANDLAGATE -- R 238 MILLION AND STILL CLIMBING."

"EXPENDITURES INCLUDE TWENTY SECURITY COTTAGES... A GIANT ENTERTAINMENT CENTRE... UNDERGROUND TUNNELS..."

"...A DOUBLE HELIPAD... AND TWO ASTROTURF SOCCER PITCHES."

©RAPID PHASE · 2012

... SIR?

SEND A LETTER TO PRESIDENT ZUMA.

GO AHEAD, SIR.

"DEAR JACOB, WAY TO GO! YOU DA MAN!"

HOW SHOULD I SIGN IT? "KIND REGARDS, PRESIDENT MUGABE?"

NAH -- JUST PUT: "WITH GREAT **ADMIRATION**, LOVE, BOB."

MADAM & Eve

BY STEPHEN FRANCIS & RICO

AND IN OTHER NEWS... THE **DISNEY** ORGANISATION HAS JUST PURCHASED THE **STAR WARS** FRANCHISE FROM **GEORGE LUCAS** FOR FOUR BILLION DOLLARS.

ACCORDING TO LATEST REPORTS, **DISNEY** IS ALSO THINKING OF BUYING THE **ANC**.

CRASH!!

MISTER PRESIDENT... ARE YOU **SURE** WE HAVE TO WEAR **THESE**?

IT'S PART OF THE **DEAL**. HOW DO YOU THINK I FEEL? I HAD TO **RESHUFFLE** MY ENTIRE CABINET!

MEET OUR NEW **MINISTER OF FINANCE**... SCROOGE McDUCK.

GRUMPY AND **DOPEY**... IN CHARGE OF OUR NEW MINE NATIONALISATION PROGRAMME.

DUMBO WILL BE RESTRUCTURING **SOUTH AFRICAN AIRWAYS**...

AND MEET OUR NEW SPIN DOCTOR... PINNOCHIO.

AND PLANS ARE ALREADY UNDERWAY TO TURN **NKANDLA** INTO A GIANT **DISNEY** THEME PARK!

UH... SIR? WHAT ABOUT INVESTIGATIONS INTO **CORRUPTION** AND **KICKBACKS**?

©RAPID PHASE - 2012

ALREADY SORTED... MEET **GOOFY**, OUR NEW **PUBLIC PROTECTOR**.

HYUK! HYUK!

... AND ON A PERSONAL NOTE, IT'S MY PLEASURE TO INTRODUCE THE FUTURE NEXT **MRS. ZUMA**!

SNOW WHITE?! HE'S PAYING **LOBOLA** FOR SNOW WHITE?!

THAT DOES IT! NO MORE CARTOON NETWORK AFTER COCKTAIL HOUR!

YOU WANTED TO SEE ME, MISTER PRESIDENT?

YES, I'M WRITING A **BOOK** AND I NEED YOUR HELP.

"APPEAR WEAK WHEN YOU ARE STRONGER. HAVE MANY WIVES AND SPEND TAXPAYER MONEY."

UH... SUN TZU? "THE ART OF WAR?"

J. ZUMA "THE ART OF POLITICS."

MAY NEED WORK, SIR.

MISTER PRESIDENT, THERE SEEMS TO BE A AT YOUR **R 240 MILLION NKANDLA** COMPOUND.

A **LEAK**?

IMPOSSIBLE! I SPENT **MILLIONS** ON FIXTURES! I PAID EXTRA FOR SHORT-CUT TENDERS!

A **FORTUNE** ON KICKBACKS AND DOUBLE-PLATED GOLD TAPS. HOW CAN THERE BE A **LEAK**?!

NOT A LEAK IN THE PLUMBING... SOMEONE'S TALKING TO THE **MEDIA**.

ARREST HIM! ... I STILL HAVE HOT WATER, DON'T I?

MISTER PRESIDENT -- YOU'VE GOT TO ISSUE A STATEMENT! THIS **NKANDLAGATE** THING IS GETTING OUT OF HAND!

DID YOU SAY "NKANDLAGATE?"

"NKANDLAGATE!" THAT **REMINDS** ME!

TELL THE CONTRACTOR TO INSTALL THE R 10 MILLION **AUTOMATIC SECURITY GATE.**

THREE! ONE, TWO, THREE!

YOU WANT TO BUY A HOTEL?

NO. I WANT TO BUY A COMPOUND.

A COMPOUND? BUT THAT COSTS 203 MILLION!!

HERE'S TWO-HUNDRED BUCKS. GET THE REST FROM THE TAXPAYERS.

ZUMA MONOPOLY. I'M UNDEFEATED.

EVE!! WHERE'S MY GIN & TONIC?!

AND IN OTHER NEWS... IN ADDITION TO THOUSANDS OF UNDELIVERED **TEXTBOOKS** IN **LIMPOPO**...

... INVESTIGATORS HAVE NOW UNCOVERED THOUSANDS OF UNDELIVERED **TEXT MESSAGES**...

...PLUS THOUSANDS OF MISSING **TEXTILES**...

... AND ANYONE ORIGINALLY FROM **TEXAS** IS ADVISED TO **LEAVE** LIMPOPO **IMMEDIATELY**.

THIS IS GETTING **WEIRD**.

:GASP:

SLAM!!

YOU LEFT VOLUNTARILY?

I'LL NEVER GET THAT **IMAGE** OUT OF MY HEAD.

...A HALF DOZEN 80 YEAR-OLD **WHITE** GOGOS DANCING TO MANDOZA'S NKALAKATHA.

STOP! I'VE HEARD ENOUGH!

MADAM & Eve

BY STEPHEN FRANCIS & RICO

NEW SOUTH AFRICAN STREET SLANG

Nkandla: (n-can-dla), n.
outrageously expensive, a waste of money

Shoe Palace

CAN YOU **BELIEVE** THE **PRICE** OF THOSE SHOES ?!

IT'S A TOTAL **NKANDLA!!**

Limpopo: (Lim-po-po), v.
to lose; to disappear mysteriously

THANDI! WHERE'S YOUR **HOMEWORK** ?!

IT'S NOT MY FAULT! IT GOT **LIMPOPOED!**

---

e-tolli: (ee-tole-ee), n.
slang for Johannesburg, South Africa

"CITY OF GOLD?" HMPH! "CITY OF **TOLLS**" IS MORE LIKE IT!

© RAPID PHASE - 2012

---

census: (sen-suss), n, adj.
nonsense; nothing adds up; losing it

PRESIDENT ZUMA'S NKANDLA COMPOUND REPORTEDLY INCLUDES A HELIPAD, AN ASTRO-TURF SOCCER PITCH AND AN UNDERGROUND BUNKER...

HE'S TAKEN LEAVE OF HIS **CENSUS.**

---

nationalise: (nah-shun-ah-lize), v.
to ruin, break or destroy

CRASH!

THAT WAS A BRAND NEW IRONING BOARD... AND YOU COMPLETELY **NATIONALISED** IT!

---

zille villa: (zill-ah vill-ah), n.
a wild goose chase; an inpenetrable area; stopped at gate; unable to continue

@#✕@.!! THE CROWBAR JUST BROKE!

CLANG!

FORGET IT. LET'S TRY SOMEWHERE ELSE! THIS PLACE IS A TOTAL **ZILLE VILLA!**

Maharaj: (mah-ha-rahj), n. **maharajing**, v.
a complete or partial falsehood: an outrageous exaggeration; weaving a fabrication

UH-OH. THERE'S THE **TRAFFIC COP**. I HOPE YOU **MAHARAJED** A BELIEVABLE STORY.

MADAM & Eve

BY STEPHEN FRANCIS & RICO

POLICE ARE TRAINING FOR A NEW LAW THAT WOULD ALLOW THEM TO **ARREST** PERPETRATORS WHO **BESMIRCH** AND **INSULT** THE PRESIDENT'S DIGNITY.

SIR... WHAT IF THE **PRESIDENT** DOES OR SAYS SOMETHING THAT INSULTS **HIMSELF**? DO WE **ARREST** HIM?

ER,... I'LL GET BACK TO YOU ON THAT ONE.

CAPTAIN-- WHAT CONSTITUTES AN ARRESTABLE ASSAULT ON THE PRESIDENT'S DIGNITY?

GOOD QUESTION.

FOR ONE, CALLING HIM A G#*G#&G... OR A *#G@*G AND A G%#*#.

WRITE THAT DOWN.

WHAT ABOUT CALLING HIM A *G&#G?

YES, I WOULD SAY THAT'S DEFINITELY ARRESTABLE.

... ALSO A G##*#, @&#*G OR A *#&*#. HOWEVER, IF SOMEONE CALLS HIM A #G$*... IT'S ONLY A SMALL CASH FINE.

AND,... ARREST ANYONE WHO PAINTS OR DISPLAYS THE PRESIDENTIAL GENITALS.

©RAPID PHASE- 2012

HOW DO WE **KNOW** IF THEY BELONG TO THE **PRESIDENT**?

GOOD QUESTION.

WE'VE HAD THEM **PHOTOGRAPHED** AND MOUNTED ON INDEX CARDS. PLEASE TAKE A STACK ON YOUR WAY OUT AND GIVE ONE TO EVERY COP YOU MEET.

REMEMBER-- PROTECTING THE PRESIDENT'S **DIGNITY** IS OUR NUMBER ONE **PRIORITY**!

HEY! IT'S IN COLOUR!

LOOKS **PHOTO-SHOPPED** TO ME.

e-TROLLS

Keep left at end of passage.

Turn right at empty ironing board.

Proceed to washer-dryer. You have reached your destination.

LET'S GO. BACK TO WORK.

I HATE THAT NEW **DOMESTIC GPS APP.**

AND WE'LL BE BACK ... WITH MORE NEWS OF **HURRICANE SANDY.**

HOW COME **WE** HARDLY EVER HAVE **HURRICANES** IN **SOUTH AFRICA?**

BECAUSE OF **WHITE PEOPLE.** WE COULD NEVER **REMEMBER** NAMES LIKE **HURRICANE SIBONAKALISO** AND **HURRICANE TSHOLOFELO.**

MOM!!

HEY! YOU HAVE A **BETTER EXPLANATION?!**

ACTUALLY... IT MAKES SENSE IN A WEIRD SORT OF WAY.

MADAM & Eve

BY STEPHEN FRANCIS & RICO

NEW REVISED SOUTH AFRICAN CLASSIC CHILDREN'S BOOKS

Harry Potter and the Chamber of State Secrets

TENDER ISLAND

THE VERY HUNGRY CATERPILLAR

WHERE THE WILD THINGS ARE

Zille in Wonderland

The MAC in the HAT

THE LITTLE GRAVY TRAIN THAT COULD

THE CHRONICLES OF NKANDLIA

I HAVE A BOND.

27

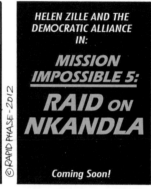

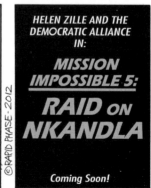

Introducing

Haagen-Daas's

new range of South African ice cream flavours!

ZILLE VANILLA

NKANDLA WASTE OF TAXPAYER MONEY!

ROCKY POTHOLE ROAD

CRUNCH!

LIMPOPO LEMON

OUT OF STOCK

WAITING FOR DELIVERY

Introducing

Haagen-Daas's

new range of South African ice cream flavours!

TAXPAYER TOFFEE

R 2500.00 PER SCOOP

STICKY FINGER MINISTER

MACADAMIA MAHARAJ BRITTLE

JISLAAIK!

UNBELIEVABLE!

JUST TAKE A LOOK AT THAT SQUANDER CAMP!

... DON'T YOU MEAN "SQUATTER CAMP?"

NO. I MEAN SQUANDER CAMP.

COMING UP... MORE ON OUR EXCLUSIVE REPORT ON NKANDLA ... PRESIDENT ZUMA'S R 248 MILLION TAXPAYER-FUNDED LUXURY ENCLOSED NEIGHBOURHOOD ... AFTER THIS.

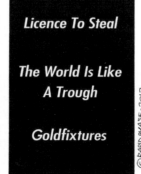

* WHO CAN BORROW **MILLIONS**? SPEND IT ON A **HOME**?

* TO THE TUNE OF "THE CANDY MAN CAN"

HELICOPTERS, BUNKERS AND TAXPAYER FREE **LOAN**?

NKANDLA MAN CAN! NKANDLA MAN CAN!

WHO CAN BUILD A **COMPOUND**? AND CALL IT ALL A **HOUSE**? WHILE OTHER PEOPLE LIVE ON FOOD THAT _BARELY_ FEEDS A **MOUSE** ...

©RAPID PHASE - 2012

SLAM! OFFICIAL **MORATORIUM** ON NKANDLA JOKES!

HEY! YOU NKANDLA DO THAT!

www.madamandeve.co.za

EVE!! YOU CALL THIS LOUNGE CLEAN?!

www.madamandeve.co.za

©RAPID PHASE - 2012

WELL, ACCORDING TO CYBERSPACE, 38 023 PEOPLE **LIKE** THE JOB I DID VACUUMING.

... AND 72 362 PEOPLE THINK I DESERVE A **RAISE** AND MORE **PAID LEAVE**.

THANKS A **LOT**, FACEBOOK!

AND 12 426 THINK YOUR PUNCHLINE COULD BE **FUNNIER**.

GUESS WHAT?!

THE **WORLD TOILET SUMMIT** IS BEING HELD THIS WEEK IN DURBAN!

www.madamandeve.co.za

SLAM!!

IT'S _TRUE_!

©RAPID PHASE - 2012

THAT'S THE TROUBLE WITH CRYING **WOLF** TOO MUCH. WHEN YOU CRY "**TOILET**", NO ONE BELIEVES YOU.

SANTA'S GROTTO

THAT'S NOT THE **REAL** FATHER CHRISTMAS, YOU KNOW. THAT'S ONE OF HIS "HELPERS."

I KNOW.

... LIKE **PRESIDENT ZUMA**. HE HAS LOTS OF "HELPERS" TOO!

SOME **HELP** HIM PAY HIS **BOND** ... SOME **HELP** HIM BUY A **CAR**, SOME ... **HEY!**

WHO ARE YOU SPYING ON?

MY MOTHER. SHE'S **DATING** FATHER CHRISTMAS.

WHAT?!

NOT REALLY. WHEN SHE TOOK THANDI TO THE MALL, THE GUY **DRESSED** AS FATHER CHRISTMAS ASKED HER OUT.

SO? WHAT'S WRONG WITH THAT?

OH.

SO. TELL ME ABOUT YOURSELF.

WHEREVER I GO, PEOPLE ARE TALKING ABOUT THE **THREE WISE MEN**!

OF COURSE, IT'S THE CHRISTMAS SEASON.

CHRISTMAS HAS **NOTHING** TO DO WITH IT.

THE **THREE WISE MEN?** BALTHAZAR, MELCHIOR, GASPAR? ON **CAMELS**?

NO... VAVI, MAHARAJ AND RAMAPHOSA.

I DON'T KNOW ABOUT **CAMELS**, BUT IT LOOKS LIKE THEY **BACKED** THE RIGHT **HORSE**.

MADAM & EVE

BY STEPHEN FRANCIS & RICO

HOHOHO! MAKE SURE YOUR HOLIDAYS **ARE** HAPPY...

...WITH MADAM & EVE'S LAST MINUTE CHRISTMAS **GIFT CATALOGUE** FOR THE BUSY POLITICIAN!

Bond repayments got you down?

Debt-All

Removes those troublesome red ink stains before you can say "GUPTA!"

Debt-All

HEY KIDS! IT'S FUN! IT BOUNCES! IT'S...

LIMPOGO!

Guaranteed to take your mind off missing textbooks!

BOING! BOING! BOING!

Allow 2 to 3 weeks for delivery. If it ever arrives.

Pfft. Pfft.

Get rid of the stench of MORAL DECAY!

Lie-sol

Lie-sol
Air Freshener

Now available in pothole-pourri.

The timeless classic fragrance for men in power

by Calvin Kleen

CORRUPTION by Calvin Kleen

CORRUPTION

©RAPID PHASE - 2012

The ULTIMATE in luxury car cleaning...

Mr. Minister

Keeps your Mercs and BMW's looking like a MILLION BUCKS!

SPECIAL CLEARANCE!

PRICED TO MOVE!

Hugely popular last year, but for some reason, popularity has plummeted. Our loss, is your gain!
ORDER NOW!!

"Motlanthe for President" t-shirts!

Sushi tables

REVOLUTIONARY BERETS
Special offer: Buy TWO berets and get a free "We Kill For Zuma" t-shirt!

38

HERE YOU GO, MADAM.

HERE, EVE. YOU GO FIRST.

"I PROMISE TO WORK HARDER."

...AND I "PROMISE TO PAY MORE MONEY."

HAHAHA!! HOHOHO!! HEE HEE HEE!

THE ANNUAL "EXCHANGE OF NEW YEAR'S RESOLUTIONS." A GREAT TRADITION.

HAHAHA!!

HOHOHO!!

HAPPY NEW YEAR!!

HONK!!

THE CHINESE SAY 2013 IS THE YEAR OF THE SNAKE! WHAT DO YOU THINK WHAT THE YEAR SHOULD BE? HUH? WHAT?

PICK SOMETHING! 2013 IS... WHAT?! SAY THE FIRST THING THAT POPS INTO YOUR HEAD! GO ON!!

WELL?

APPARENTLY IT'S THE YEAR OF "GO PLAY OUTSIDE-- I HAVE A HANGOVER."

CLINK!
CLINK!
CLINK!

CLINK!
CLINK!
CLINK!
CLINK!

©RAPID PHASE-2013

CRASH!
CLATTER!
TINKLE!
CLINK!

POST-HOLIDAYS RECYCLING.

LOOK AT ALL THIS STRANGE **FOLIAGE** THAT HAS GROWN IN OUR GARDEN DURING THE **HOLIDAYS**.

©RAPID PHASE - 2013

WHAT'S THE NAME OF THAT **MOVIE MUSICAL** WITH THE **GIANT PLANT** THAT **EATS** PEOPLE?

www.madamandeve.co.za

LITTLE SHOP OF HORRORS. ...IT'S ONE OF MY FAVOURITES.

MINE TOO.

MINE TOO.

WHEN DOES THE **GARDENER** GET **BACK** AGAIN?!

TUESDAY!

FEED ME.

HEY BOB! WELCOME BACK!

HOW WAS YOUR HOLIDAY?

NOT BAD. YOURS?

GREAT.

IT'S NOT GOING TO BE EASY... GETTING **BACK** INTO THE DAILY GRIND.

YOU CAN SAY THAT AGAIN. WELL... BETTER GET TO **WORK.**

©RAPID PHASE - 2013   www.madamandeve.co.za

NO WORK NO FOOD

NO JOB NO MONEY

NOOOO.!! THIS CAN'T BE RIGHT!

WHY IS THIS HAPPENING TO ME?!

THIS IS SO UNFAIR!!

I HATE MY LIFE!!

FIRST DAY BACK AT SCHOOL AFTER THE HOLIDAYS?

YEP.

© RAPID PHASE - 2013

www.madamandeve.co.za

TWEET!!

SLAM!

SLAM!

SLAM!

SLAM!

"...AND THAT'S HOW I SPENT MY CHRISTMAS HOLIDAYS. THE END."

CLAP! CLAP! CLAP! CLAP! CLAP!

YOU'RE SO LUCKY. MY PARENTS MADE ME GO TO THE KRUGER PARK.

www.madamandeve.co.za

©RAPID PHASE - 2013

WELL?! GO ON!!

WHAT ARE YOU WAITING FOR?!!

www.madamandeve.co.za

IT GOES ON FOR ANOTHER FEW SECONDS, BUT YOU GET THE IDEA.

©RAPID PHASE - 2013

I MAY HAVE OVERESTIMATED THE DEMAND FOR A "GET OUT OF MY CLASS AND GO TO THE PRINCIPAL'S OFFICE" SMARTPHONE APP.

PRINCIPA

MADAM & Eve

BY STEPHEN FRANCIS & RICO

AND IN OTHER NEWS... EX ANCYL PRESIDENT *JULIUS MALEMA* SAYS NOT TO "COUNT HIM OUT"... BECAUSE IT "AIN'T OVER UNTIL THE **FAT LADY** SINGS "...

... AND WAKES UP, EATS BREAKFAST, AND YOU PAY FOR THE FAT LADY'S TAXI IN THE MORNING.

MOM!!

No one is taking his calls.

His friends and allies have abandoned him in droves.

He's down ... but not _out_.

Out but not _down_.

And whatever it takes, he'll be back, because ...

HUH?

©RAPID PHASE - 2013

HEY! COME BACK WITH MY **BERET** YOU ⓖ✱#ⓖ URCHIN!

Le Misérable Malema

COMING BACK SOON ... OR MAYBE NOT.

ONCE I'D KILL FOR ZUMA!! ♪

NOW HE'S NOT MORE THAN A RUMOUR!!

WE WERE SALT AND PEPPER! ♪

NOW THEY TREAT ME LIKE A LEPER!! ♪

I GOT THE ♪ OL' ANC YOUTH LEAGUE BLUES!! ♪

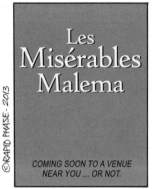

Les Misérables Malema

COMING SOON TO A VENUE NEAR YOU ... OR NOT.

THEY SAY JULIUS MALEMA WAS BROUGHT DOWN BY KARMA.

"KARMA."

I'M THINKING OF JOINING KARMA. WHAT'S THEIR POLITICAL AFFILIATION AND DO THEY HAVE A YOUTH LEAGUE?!

FINE! KEEP THE ORGANISATION SECRET! SEE IF I CARE!!

AND IN OTHE NEWS, PRESIDENT ZUMA VOWS TO DISPEL THE "UNFAIR MYTH" THAT EVERY ANC CADRE IS CORRUPT.

MISTER PRESIDENT... THAT'S A TALL ORDER. MAYBE WE SHOULD START SMALL.

SMALL?

CONVINCE PEOPLE THAT ONLY EVERY OTHER ANC CADRE IS CORRUPT. THEN WE HAVE SOMETHING TO WORK TOWARD.

I LIKE IT! TELL OUR P.R. COMPANY TO RUN WITH IT!

WHICH P.R. FIRM, SIR? THE ONE OWNED BY YOUR THIRD WIFE'S COUSIN'S BROTHER? ... OR THE ONE OF YOUR AUNT'S SISTER'S NEIGHBOUR?

OH, FOR @*#@ SAKE -- JUST PICK ONE.

www.madamandeve.co.za ©RAPID PHASE - 2013

AND IN OTHER NEWS, A LAVISH **65 MILLION RAND** WAS SPENT **RENOVATING** MINISTERS' HOMES THIS PAST YEAR. THE GOVERNMENT DEFENDED THIS EXPENDITURE, CLAIMING...

...IT'S A LEGITIMATE EXPENSE AND OUTLINED IN THE CURRENT MINISTERIAL HANDOUT BOOK.

www.madamandeve.co.za

...ER, "HANDBOOK." THE MINISTERIAL HANDBOOK.

HEE HEE.

©RAPID PHASE–2013

...IN TODAY'S HEADLINES, CYCLIST **LANCE ARMSTRONG** HAS FINALLY ADMITTED TO USING BANNED DRUGS...

WHAT A **DOPE!** CAN'T ANYBODY DO ANYTHING THESE DAYS WITHOUT **PERFORMANCE ENHANCING SUBSTANCES?!**

©RAPID PHASE–2013

MIELLLIES!!

GULP!!

MIELLLIES!!

DRUG FREE DOMESTIC PERFORMANCE ENHANCEMENT

Only 10 Rand

OKAY, HERE'S MY TEN BUCKS. WHAT'S THE **SECRET** OF **DRUG-FREE DOMESTIC PERFORMANCE ENHANCEMENT?**

WAGE INCREASE.

©RAPID PHASE–2013   www.madamandeve.co.za

WAIT! I WASN'T DONE! A **PAID VACATION** WORKS TOO!!

DRUG FREE DOMESTIC PERFORMANCE ENHANCEMENT Only 10 Rand

Panel 1: (silent)

PERFORMANCE ENHANCING LEMONADE R5

Panel 2: PERFORMANCE ENHANCING LEMONADE R5

Panel 3: PERFORMANCE ENHANCING LEMONADE

Panel 4: I BET SHE'S NEVER RUN **THAT** FAST BEFORE. WE'RE ALMOST OUT OF **CHILI** POWDER.

PERFORMANCE ENHANCING LEMONADE R5

Panel 5: AND IN OTHER NEWS....

Panel 6: PRESIDENT ZUMA HAS ORDERED IMMEDIATE **TESTING** OF ALL GOVERNMENT OFFICIALS TO DETERMINE THE PRESENCE OF **PERFORMANCE ENHANCING** DRUGS.

Panel 7: WITH THE TESTING ALMOST COMPLETE, IT'S CLEAR THAT NOT **ONE** OFFICIAL IS TAKING PERFORMANCE ENHANCING DRUGS.

Panel 8: HOWEVER, NUMEROUS MINISTERS TESTED POSITIVE FOR PERFORMANCE **DECREASING** DRUGS.

Panel 9: AND, IN AFRICAN CUP OF NATIONS SOCCER NEWS... NATIONAL TEAM MANAGEMENT CLAIM MORALE IS AT AN ALL TIME **HIGH** ...AND THEY HAVE **GOOD** NEWS AND **BAD** NEWS.

Panel 10: ‹AHEM› WE'VE TESTED EVERY MEMBER OF BAFANA BAFANA AND NOT **ONE PLAYER** IS USING PERFORMANCE ENHANCING DRUGS!

GOOD NEWS.

Panel 11: THAT'S THE **BAD** NEWS. THE **GOOD** NEWS IS THAT WE'VE PUT "PREFERRED STEROID SUPPLIER" OUT TO TENDER... AND THE RESULTS ARE OVERWHELMINGLY POSITIVE.

Panel 12: WE'VE LEVELED THE PLAYING FIELD AND WE'RE BACK IN THE GAME!

BAFANA! BAFANA! BAFANA!

MADAM & Eve

BY STEPHEN FRANCIS & RICO

AND IN OTHER NEWS, PRESIDENT ZUMA HAS COMMISSIONED A RESEARCH PAPER ON "PERFORMANCE ENHANCEMENT"... IN AN EFFORT TO IMPROVE THE PERFORMANCE OF GOVERNMENT OFFICIALS.

ZUMA SAYS THAT THE PROJECT SHOULD HAVE BEEN FINISHED BY NOW, BUT IS TAKING A LONG TIME DUE TO THE FACT THAT THE PERFORMANCE OF THE EXPERTS INVESTIGATING PERFORMANCE ENHANCEMENT NEEDS TO BE GREATLY ENHANCED.

GOOD NEWS, MISTER PRESIDENT! THAT RESEARCH PAPER YOU COMMISSIONED ON PERFORMANCE ENHANCEMENT IS FINALLY FINISHED!

ABOUT TIME! GIVE ME THE SHORT VERSION!

NUMBER ONE: "PERFORMANCE CAN BE ENHANCED BY ILLEGAL DRUGS."

FORGET IT. TOO EASY TO SPOT. NEXT!

NUMBER TWO: "PERFORMANCE CAN BE ENHANCED BY HARD WORK, TRANSPARENCY, INTEGRITY, FAIRNESS, SERVICE DELIVERY AND HONESTY."

...WHAT'S NUMBER THREE?

NUMBER THREE: "WE COOK THE BOOKS, EXAGGERATE THE FIGURES AND TELL EVERYONE WE'RE DOING ONE HECK OF A JOB."

HMM.

©RAPID PHASE - 2013

...I'M LEANING TOWARDS NUMBER THREE.

WHEW! ME TOO!

TALK ABOUT A NO-BRAINER!

WORKS FOR ME!

I NEED A DRINK!

We help because we believe that where there's help there's a way.

And where there's a way it's always helpful to believe there's help.

Because after all the pressure, nobody knows <u>what</u> we believe or what we're talking about. And neither do we.

www.madamandeve.co.za

© RAPID PHASE - 2013

Do you? Then you can help us help you to help us.

(before we all lose our jobs)

FNB

THIS MESSAGE ENDORSED BY THE ANC.

WOW. THE ANC ARE REALLY MEAN.

THEY CALL ONE OF THEIR OWN MEMBERS THE "ANC CHIEF WIMP."

I UNDER-STAND THEY ALSO HAVE A **DEPUTY** CHIEF WIMP.

WHIP!! NOT "WIMP." WHIP!!

© RAPID PHASE - 2013

www.madamandeve.co.za

WE WERE WRONG. IT'S JUST "ANC BULLWHIP."

I HEARD THAT ALSO.

AND IN OTHER NEWS, THE SOUTH AFRICAN REVENUE SERVICE HAS FILED PAPERS DEMANDING THAT JULIUS MALEMA BE **SEQUESTRATED.**

www.madamandeve.co.za

WOW.

THE TAXMAN'S GOING TO **SEQUESTRATE** MALEMA.

© RAPID PHASE - 2013

THEY CAN DO THAT?!

I GUESS THEY'RE GETTING REALLY **STRICT** ABOUT SEIZING HIS **ASSETS.**

YOU THINK HIS SPEECHES WILL BE IN FALSETTO?

...YOU'RE GOING TO **TELL** THEM, RIGHT?

MAYBE AFTER MY TEA BREAK.

MADAM & Eve

BY STEPHEN FRANCIS & RICO

To remind us who we are, we asked the children of South Africa. We wanted to know how they feel about the future.

AND... **ACTION!!**

CUT!

WHAT WAS THAT?!

MY EMOTION-FILLED WALK TO THE PODIUM. I'M TRYING TO ADD A LITTLE MORE **DRAMA**.

IT'S FINE AS IT IS. JUST TRY AND BE YOURSELF. AND... **ACTION!!**

"THERE WILL BE A DAY... A DAY WHEN THE DIFFICULTIES WE SEE BEFORE US -- THE GREED, MISTRUST AND..."

WHO WROTE THIS STUFF?!

JUST KEEP GOING!

BECAUSE ... A DAY MAY COME WHEN OUR COURAGE FAILS ... BUT IT IS **NOT THIS DAY!** WHEN WE FORSAKE ALL BONDS OF FELLOWSHIP -- BUT IT IS **NOT THIS DAY!**

CUT!! WHAT THE HELL WAS **THAT**?!

IT'S THE FINAL SPEECH FROM **LORD OF THE RINGS**. NOW **THAT'S** WHAT I CALL INSPIRATIONAL!

© RAPID PHASE · 2013

INCIDENTALLY, THERE'S NOTHING EVEN **HERE** ABOUT "NKANDLA" OR THE "ARMS DEAL!" ... YOU WANT ME TO DO A QUICK **REWRITE**?!

NEXT!!

WAIT! I'M JUST GETTING **WARMED UP!!**

SO. HOW DID YOUR AUDITION GO?

I THINK I TOTALLY **NAILED** IT!

WHAT ARE YOU DOING?

I'M PREPARING MY PROPOSAL TO THE **GUPTA BROTHERS.**

I READ THAT THEY'RE **GIVING MONEY** AWAY! NOT JUST TO THE **ANC** -- BUT TO **EVERYONE.**

*... AND THEY EXPECT NOTHING IN RETURN. I'M GETTING IN ON THE **GROUND FLOOR** BEFORE SOMEBODY **WISES UP.***

I SEE YOU'RE GOING WITH POWER-POINT.

I'LL BE NEEDING A BRIEF BUT GLOWING TESTIMONIAL.

YOU WANTED TO SEE ME, COUNCILMAN VUSI?

YES. TAKE A LETTER.

"DEAR **GUPTA** BROTHERS, SINCE YOU'RE ALREADY HANDING IT OUT, PLEASE CONSIDER GIVING **ME** LOTS OF MONEY. AND I'LL GIVE YOU (AHEM)... '**NOTHING**' IN RETURN."

YOU WANT ME TO PUT THE "(AHEM)" IN, SIR?

ABSOLUTELY.

*"...AND I'LL GIVE YOU (AHEM) **NOTHING** IN RETURN. WINK, WINK. NUDGE, NUDGE. SIGNED, COUNCILMAN VUSI."* ... AND ADD A **SMILEY FACE** AFTER MY NAME.

GENIUS, SIR.

HMPH. "CELEBRITIES." THEY'RE ALWAYS GETTING "**WHISKED**" SOMEWHERE.

HUH?

LISTEN TO THIS: "RAPPER **KANYE WEST** ARRIVED AT O.R. TAMBO AIRPORT... AND WAS IMMEDIATELY **WHISKED** AWAY!"

WHAT DOES **THAT** MEAN? DID HIS MINDER **YANK** HIM INTO A **LIMO**? WAS HE **PULLED** BY A **BUNGI CORD?!** HOW DO YOU "**WHISK**" SOMEONE AWAY?!

SLAM!!

EVEN **I** SAW THAT ONE COMING.

GREAT NEWS. I'M RUNNING FOR STUDENT BODY PRESIDENT.

CONGRATULATIONS.

VOTE THANDI

...CARE TO MAKE A **CONTRIBUTION** TO MY CAMPAIGN?

I DON'T KNOW. WHAT'S YOUR **PLATFORM**?

NO HOMEWORK. LONGER BREAKS. MORE HOLIDAYS AND EXTENDED LUNCH TIME.

FINE! AND SAY GOODBYE TO **YOUR** CHANCE OF WINNING THE **TUCK SHOP** TENDER!

HI. HI... GOOD TO SEE YOU. HIYA. ...HI.

VOTE THANDI SISULU STUDENT BODY PRESIDENT

HELLO. I'M VERY IMPRESSED. PLEASE ACCEPT **R20** FOR YOUR CAMPAIGN.

SERIOUSLY?

...AND NO STRINGS ATTACHED. I JUST ENJOY HANDING OUT MONEY TO PEOPLE OF FUTURE INFLUENCE.

WHO **WAS** THAT KID?

HIS SURNAME'S **GUPTA**.

HELLO. I'M VERY IMPRESSED.

AND IN OTHER NEWS... ONCE **AGAIN**, SCHOOLS IN **LIMPOPO** HAVE **NOT** RECEIVED THEIR **TEXTBOOKS** FOR THIS YEAR!

UNBELIEVABLE!! NOT **THIS** AGAIN?!

DOESN'T ANYONE IN LIMPOPO KNOW THE **MEANING** OF **DEJA VU**?!!

... SOME OF THE BOOKS STILL MISSING, INCLUDE WEBSTER'S ENGLISH DICTIONARY.

MADAM & Eve

BY STEPHEN FRANCIS & RICO

READY FOR YOUR FIRST CHALLENGE, MISTER MINISTER?

YEBO! FIRE AWAY!

"MISTER MINISTER?"

WHAT IMPORTANT DOCUMENT IS KNOWN AS THE "CORNERSTONE OF **DEMOCRACY** IN SOUTH AFRICA?"

a. THE BILL OF RIGHTS?

b. THE SECRECY BILL?

c. THE MINISTERIAL HANDBOOK?

WAIT. I **KNOW** THIS ONE!

TAKE YOUR TIME...THE "CORNERSTONE OF DEMOCRACY."

c. THE MINISTERIAL HANDBOOK.

UH... IS THIS YOUR **FINAL** ANSWER?

YEP!

...YOU **SURE**? YOU WANT TO MAYBE **THINK** ABOUT IT SOME MORE? TO BE **SURE** YOU'RE **RIGHT**?...SO YOU CAN CHOOSE THE **RIGHT** ONE, MISTER MINISTER.

© RAPID PHASE - 2013

NO - THAT'S MY FINAL ANSWER: C. THE MINISTERIAL HANDBOOK.

I'M SORRY...THAT'S **INCORRECT**.

...BUT YOU CAME SO **CLOSE**, WE'RE **GIVING YOU** THE **MILLION BUCKS ANYWAY!!**

NO STRINGS ATTACHED!!

★ ★ ★
WHO WANTS TO BE A
MILLIONAIRE
IN GOVERNMENT?
★ ★ ★

A Gupta Brothers Production

Coming soon to a SABC channel near you!

54

MADAM & Eve

BY STEPHEN FRANCIS & RICO

ARE YOU READY WITH YOUR RESEARCH PAPER, THANDI?

YES, MISS.

AHEM. "HOW TO CHOSE A NEW POPE." BY THANDI SISULU

"CHOOSING A NEW POPE ISN'T **EASY**. THERE ARE MANY THINGS THE **JUDGES** MUST CONSIDER."

JUDGES?

"THE TENSION BEGINS AS POTENTIAL POPES AUDITION AND ARE SHORTLISTED."

"QUALITIES SUCH AS PERSONALITY, CHARISMA, STYLE AND FASHION SENSE ARE VERY IMPORTANT."

" ... AND, OF COURSE, TALENT."

TALENT?

"FINALLY, AFTER ALL THE CONDITIONS ARE MET AND THE CLOCK TICKS DOWN... IT'S TIME FOR THE **BIG DAY**."

" ... AND THE FIRST EPISODE OF **POPE IDOLS** IS BROADCAST."

POPE IDOLS

"FROM THEN ON, IT'S UP TO THE JUDGES AND THE GENERAL **PUBLIC** WHO SMS THEIR **VOTE** FOR THE WINNING POPE."

THANK YOU.

WHAT MAKES YOU THINK I DIDN'T DO THE **RESEARCH**?!

PRINCIPAL

FOLLOWING HIS SURPRISE RESIGNATION, **POPE BENEDICT XVI** PLANS TO TRAVEL THE WORLD, LOOKING FOR A COUNTRY IN WHICH HE CAN **RETIRE** QUIETLY.

HEY! MAYBE HE'LL SETTLE IN SOUTH AFRICA?

SORRY TO INTERRUPT **SCHABIR**, BUT A PARTY OF **VIP'S** NEED TO PLAY THROUGH.

HMPH. TOURISTS.

I'D TRY THE FIVE IRON, YOUR HOLINESS.

FREEZE! ARMED RESPONSE!!
KEEP THOSE CHERUBY HANDS WHERE WE CAN SEE THEM AND KICK THAT QUIVER OVER HERE!

Happy Valentine's Day

♡ ♡ ♡

from

Madam & Eve

BLAH. BLAH. BLAH.
BLAH. BLAH. BLAH.
BLAH. BLAH. BLAH.

BEEP! BEEP!

CHECK IT OUT: IT'S MY NEW PHONE APP: "MADAM TRACKER."

Madam approaching. Leave your current location now.

EVE! YOU DIDN'T **FINISH** THE LAUNDRY!

Turn left at first door. Keep going.

EVE?!

Recalculating...

HEY! I THINK I'VE **SOLVED** IT! IT WAS...

MISTER **OSCAR** IN THE **BEDROOM** WITH THE **REVOLVER!**

NO **WAY!**

...THE INVESTIGATING **OFFICER** IN THE **BATHROOM** WITH THE **SHOE** COVERS!

COLONEL MUSTARD IN THE KITCHEN...

PROFESSOR PLUM!

AT THE FIRING RANGE

BLAM! BLAM! BLAM! BLAM!

BLAM! BLAM! BLAM!

BLAM! BLAM! BLAM!

BLAM! BLAM! BLAM!

AND, AS MORE DETAILS EMERGE, IT'S BEGINNING TO APPEAR THAT THE **STAR ATHLETE**... HAD A HIDDEN **DARK SIDE**...

WHY ARE YOU LOOKING AT ME LIKE THAT? WHAT-- YOU THINK I HAVE A HIDDEN **DARK SIDE?**

...I WAS THINKING MORE OF A HIDDEN **NICE** SIDE.

SLAM?!

TOUCHED A **NERVE**, DIDN'T I?!

58

THE RAINBOW NATION

MADAM & Eve

BY STEPHEN FRANCIS & RICO

It began in MIAMI.

Then ... NEW YORK CITY.

And now ...
JOHANNESBURG.

CRIME SCENE INVESTIGATION: JOHANNESBURG

COMING SOON TO SABC 3.

KEEP CALM AND START A NEW POLITICAL PARTY

KEEP CALM AND *WE'LL LAND THE AIRPLANE ANYWHERE WE WANT!*

Eskom

KEEP CALM AND LIGHT SOME CANDLES

KEEP CALM AND SCORE AN OWN GOAL AND NOT QUALIFY FOR THE WORLD CUP

DA

KEEP CALM AND LOOK OUT FOR FLYING P**P

LIMPOPO

KEEP CALM AND BE PATIENT, THOSE TEXTBOOKS ARE ON THEIR WAY

KEEP CALM AND QUOTE THE MINISTERIAL HANDBOOK

JMPD

KEEP CALM AND AND BUY ME A COOLDRINK

KEEP CALM AND BUILD A R300 MILLION COMPOUND, KEEP FIRING THE NPA PROSECUTOR, STAY FRIENDS WITH THE GUPTAS, AVOID TRANSPARENCY, PASS THE SECRECY ACT... AND START LOOKING FOR YOUR NEXT WIFE

©RAPID PHASE - 2013

KEEP CALM AND HAVE ANOTHER GIN & TONIC

MADAM & Eve

BY STEPHEN FRANCIS & RICO

'TWAS THE NIGHT BEFORE CHRISTMAS AND ALL THROUGH THE ~~COMPOUND~~ RESIDENCE,

NOT A CREATURE WAS STIRRING, NOT EVEN THE PRESIDENT.

THE WIVES WERE ALL NESTLED ALL SNUG IN THEIR BEDS,

WHILE VISIONS OF GUCCI DANCED IN THEIR HEADS.

AND THEN, WHEN THE CLOCK STRUCK TWELVE LATE THAT NIGHT...

JACOB RAN TO HIS BUNKER, HE GOT SUCH A FRIGHT!

THREE **SPIRITS** APPEARED (AS HIS JAW DROPPED, AGHAST) ...THE **GHOSTS** OF ANC PRESENT, **FUTURE** AND PAST!

THE GHOST FROM THE **PAST** SPOKE "MADIBA AND BIKO -- WHO PURSUED FREEDOM AND JUSTICE --NOT FEEDING THEIR EGO!"

THEN THE GHOST FROM THE **PRESENT** DEMANDED THE FLOOR, TALKING "TENDERS AND ARMS DEALS, CORRUPTION GALORE!"

"...MISSING TEXTBOOKS, NKANDLA, DANGLING PORTRAITS AND MORE."

FATHER CHRISTMAS APPEARED, "STOP BEING A DOPE!" (HE BROUGHT MADAM AND MAID WITH A MESSAGE OF HOPE.)

THE FUTURE'S NOT WRITTEN! IT'S STILL A BLANK SLATE!

YOU CAN STILL **CHANGE** YOUR WAYS, IT'S NEVER TOO LATE!

AND THEY HEARD SOMEONE SHOUT, AS HE FLEW OFF TO LEAVE...

OUCH.

CRASH!

ZUMAVILLE

PEACE ON EARTH, HAPPY HOLIDAYS! FROM MADAM & EVE

MOM! IT'S RUBBISH COLLECTION DAY! WHERE'S YOUR EMPTY GLASS BOTTLES?!

CLINK! CLINK! CLINK! CLINK!

...REMIND YOU OF ANYTHING?

CLUCK! TINKLE! CLINK! CLINK!

©RAPID PHASE · 2013

AFRICAN DUNG BEETLE?

I HEARD THAT!!

CLINK! CLINK! CLINK!

www.madamandeve.co.za

www.madamandeve.co.za ©RAPID PHASE · 2013

EVE!! HELP!!

COMING, MADAM!!

©RAPID PHASE · 2013

THANKS. WHEN IS THE GARDENER COMING BACK FROM HOLIDAY?

NEXT TUESDAY.

SOUNDS GOOD. HOW DO I KNOW THEY REALLY WORK?

VOODOO DOLLS

GET REVENGE!

Only 20 Rand

©RAPID PHASE · 2013

OW!! MY HEAD HURTS!!

POKE!

www.madamandeve.co.za

NO MORE CHEAP GIN FOR ME.

NICE TRY.

WHAT? STILL NOT CONVINCED?

AVANT-GARDE

AVANT-CAR GUARD

AVANT-BODYGUARD

AVANT-GOGO

©RAPID PHASE - 2012

www.madamandeve.co.za

WHERE ARE YOU GOING?

TO A FUNERAL.

SADLY, OUR TRUSTED NEIGHBOURHOOD **SECURITY GUARD** PASSED AWAY. COME AND JOIN US.

©RAPID PHASE - 2012   www.madamandeve.co.za

DON'T ASK. ALL WE KNOW, IS THAT WE WOKE UP ONE MORNING, AND THERE IT WAS.

www.madamandeve.co.za

AND DO YOU KNOW ANYONE WITH A **BAKKIE?** IF YOU CART THIS **DEAD GIANT** AWAY, YOU CAN KEEP IT.

©RAPID PHASE - 2012

THIS IS THE **LAST** TIME I GO ON **LEAVE** FOR MORE THAN TWO WEEKS.

BRR RRRR RRRRA

67

Go ahead. Indulge yourself.

When you're the president ...

... life is sweet.

NKANDLEREL

Artificially sweetened non-existent bond repayments.

THE CHANGING LANDSCAPE

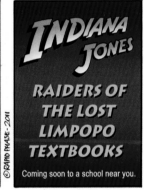

HELLO, EVE? WE'LL BE HOME SOON. MOM'S TAKING HER DRIVING TEST TO RENEW HER DRIVER'S LICENCE.

AGAIN?

DID SHE PASS?

HOLD ON...

SCREECH!!

LET ME GET BACK TO YOU ON THAT ONE.

POPULAR SOUTH AFRICAN CARD GAMES

SOLITAIRE

HOME AFFAIRS

GO PHISH

GIN RUMMY

THE STAGES OF GRIEF WHEN DISCOVERING YOU JUST MISSED A HALF-PRICE SHOE SALE.

:GASP: I MISSED THE HALF-PRICE SHOE SALE!!

SHOES

HALF PRICE SHOE SALE!

SALE OVER!

DISBELIEF

I CAN'T BELIEVE I JUST MISSED A HALF-PRICE SHOE SALE!

LUX SHO

HA PRI SALE

BARGAIN HUNTING FOR NEXT SALE

SHOULDN'T THAT BE BARGAINING?

COMING SOON! Shoe Sale! 30% OFF!!

Panel 1: IF THERE'S SOMETHING **LOUD** IN YOUR NEIGHBOURHOOD... WHO YOU GONNA CALL?

Panel 2: **MIELIE BUSTERS!!**

©RAPID PHASE-2012   www.madamandeve.co.za

Panel 3: IF IT DRAWS A CROWD... IN YOUR NEIGHBOURHOOD ... WHO YOU GONNA CALL?

B222T!

Panel 4: **MIELIE BUSTERS**

ASK US ABOUT OUR SENIOR CITIZEN DISCOUNT!

HALF-BAKED

HALF-FULL

©RAPID PHASE-2012

HALF-TOASTED

HALF DAY

Panel: **CLANG!! CLATTER!!**

WHAT WAS **THAT?!**

RELAX, MOM! IT'S JUST THE **DUSTBIN MEN!**

Panel: HMPH. WHY DO THEY CALL THEM "DUSTBINS"? ... YOU NEVER SEE ANY **DUST.**

WHAT WOULD **YOU** CALL THEM?

Panel: "PLASTIC CURBSIDE WASTE CONTAINERS ATTENDED BY IRRITATINGLY LOUD AND INCONSIDERATE ENTITIES ARRIVING DURING THE CHERISHED NAP TIMES OF INNOCENT SENIOR CITIZENS!"

©RAPID PHASE-2013   www.madamandeve.co.za

Panel: I'LL CALL THE **OXFORD DICTIONARY** AND TELL THEM TO **STOP PRESS** ON THE NEXT REPRINT.

I **HEARD** THAT!

73

THE EXPENDABLES 3

MALEMA | CELE | MBEKI | SELEBI | SHAIK | PIKOLI

MY SCHOOL HISTORY BOOK STATES THAT DURING APARTHEID, MANY FREETHINKERS PREFERRED EXILE TO REMAINING.

WHAT'S "EXILE?"

...WELL?

SLAM!!

SOMETIMES I THINK I'M TOO INQUISITIVE.

Close encounters of the third kind: Contact with Alien beings.

Hi.

Close encounters of the fourth kind: Abduction by Alien beings.

HELP!

Close encounters of the fifth kind: Alien beings inexplicably steal your homework.

HEY!

Close encounters of the sixth kind: School principal is actually an Alien.

FINE! DON'T BELIEVE ME!

PRINCIPAL

74

MADAM & Eve

BY STEPHEN FRANCIS & RICO

AND IN OTHER NEWS, A NEW STUDY AT STELLENBOSCH UNIVERSITY FOUND THAT **68%** OF ALL **BURGERS**, MINCE AND SAUSAGES CONTAINED DONKEY, **GOAT** AND **BUFFALO** MEAT.

...HOW'S YOUR BURGER?

DONKEY-GATE AND GOAT-GATE! WHO KNOWS HOW WIDESPREAD THIS IS? IT COULD GO ALL THE WAY TO THE **TOP**!

RONALD **McDONALD** HAD A **FARM**! EI EI OH! AND ON THIS FARM HE HAD A --

DONKEY!

...EI EI OH! WITH A **HEE-HAW** HERE... AND A **HEE-HAW** THERE!

DO YOU MIND?!!

SORRY. WE WERE JUST VISUALISING A **McDONKEY** QUARTER-POUNDER.

OR HOW ABOUT SOME **GOAT** McNUGGETS?!

BUT HEY, DON'T LET US PUT YOU **OFF** YOUR BURGER.

YOU'RE PROBABLY ONE OF THE LUCKY **32% MINORITY** TO GET **REAL** BEEF.

WHAT KIND OF A BURGER **IS** IT ANYWAY?

...MONKEY GLAND.

©RAPID PHASE - 2013

HOO! HOO! HOO!

HOO! HOO! HOO!

WHO **SAYS** THERE'S NO SUCH THING AS A **FREE** LUNCH?

...YOU GOING TO EAT HER PICKLE?

AND WE'LL BE BACK WITH MORE ON OUR REPORT ON **FOOD MISLABELING**...

I DON'T KNOW WHAT THE **BIG DEAL** IS ABOUT EATING GOAT OR DONKEY...

... ACCORDING TO THIS ARTICLE, THE AVERAGE PERSON SWALLOWS 4-6 **SPIDERS** PER YEAR WHILE **SLEEPING!**

SLAM?!

FINE! NEXT TIME I'LL SUGAR-COAT IT!

LUNCH IS SERVED.

ARE YOU ABSOLUTELY **SURE** THERE'S NO GOAT OR DONKEY IN THIS?

ABSOLUTELY.

IT'S **BAKED BEANS** AND **CABBAGE**.

DAMNED IF YOU **DO**...

... AND DAMNED IF YOU **DON'T.**

I'M TAKING THE AFTERNOON OFF.

FARMER BOB'S BURGERS

GUARANTEED 100% GOAT-FREE 100% DONKEY-FREE

HOW CAN YOU BE **SURE** THESE BURGERS ARE GOAT AND DONKEY-FREE?

EASY! I MAKE THE MINCE **MYSELF!**

... AND I DON'T ALLOW GOATS AND DONKEYS EVEN **NEAR** MY ABATTOIR.

BESIDES... IT MAKES THE HORSES NERVOUS.

PTOO!!

MADAM & Eve

BY STEPHEN FRANCIS & RICO

TODAY'S TOP STORY... IN LIGHT OF THE RECENT SPATE OF **POLICE BRUTALITY**, THE **SAPS** WILL BE SENDING ALL POLICE OFFICERS ON AN **ANGER MANAGEMENT** AND **SENSITIVITY** COURSE.

RIGHT! QUESTION 1: UNDER WHAT CIRCUMSTANCES WOULD YOU **DRAG** A SUSPECT BEHIND YOUR POLICE CAR?

HMM. Ooo

WAIT. I KNOW THIS ONE.

THE CORRECT ANSWER IS **NONE**! UNDER **NO** CIRCUMSTANCES WOULD YOU DO THAT!

EVEN IF HE'S **GUILTY**?

©RAPID PHASE - 2013

NEXT QUESTION: "**EXCESSIVE FORCE**" IS OFTEN USED BY _____?

JEDI KNIGHTS!

OBI WAN KENOBI!

YODA!

LET'S **FORGET** THE QUESTIONS AND TRY A BIT OF "ROLE PLAYING". YOU TWO CAN BE **POLICE OFFICER** ... AND **YOU** CAN BE THE ALLEGED SUSPECT.

... I WASN'T FINISHED YET.

AAAH! HELP!!

BONK! POW! CRUNCH! PUNCH! POW!

KICK!

:SIGH: OKAY, LET'S TRY **THIS**. EVERYBODY **TAKE ONE** AND KEEP IT WITH YOU AT ALL TIMES!

AND WHENEVER YOU'RE ON DUTY AND FEEL **FRUSTRATED** AND **AGGRESSIVE** ... TAKE YOUR **ANGER** OUT ON THIS SOFT, FLUFFY PILLOW.

YEE-HAH! WHOO-HOO!

POLICE

VROOOM!!

BONK! BONK! BONK! BONK!

WELL, TO BE HONEST, SIR ... THIS MAY TAKE A LITTLE **LONGER** THAN WE THOUGHT.

DRRRING!! ♫

WELL, THAT'S IT, CLASS. THE **EASTER LONG WEEKEND** HAS OFFICIALLY STARTED. SEE YOU ALL IN **FOUR** WHOLE DAYS!

YAY!!

YAY!!

BUNNY CHOW

BUNNY CHOW

EASTER BUNNY CHOW

www.madamandeve.co.za   © RAPID PHASE - 2013

THE **EASTER** HOLIDAYS ARE OVER! AREN'T YOU GOING TO **EAT** YOUR LEFTOVER **CHOCOLATE BUNNY?**

HELP! HELP! SHE'S **BITING** OFF MY **HEAD**!! AAAAAH!! MY HEAD!!

MY TAIL!! NOW SHE'S **EATING** MY **TAIL**!! AAAAH!!

© RAPID PHASE - 2013   www.madamandeve.co.za

SLAM!!

IT'S ONE OF OUR ANNUAL EASTER TRADITIONS. WANT TO SPLIT THE **TORSO?**

YOU'RE WEIRD.

VRRRRRRRR!

VRRRRRRR!

"REMOTE CONTROL DRONE VACUUM."

Target aquired.

SOMEBODY HELP!! IT'S SUCKING UP MY BIG TOE!!

STILL WORKING OUT A FEW MINOR BUGS.

URRRR!

AND IN OTHER NEWS, **ESKOM** MANAGEMENT WERE DELIGHTED WITH THE RESPONSE TO **"EARTH HOUR"**, WITH MILLIONS TURNING OFF POWER ON SATURDAY NIGHT TO HELP FIGHT **CLIMATE CHANGE.**

ESKOM PROMISES TO CONTINUE THEIR **SUPPORT** OF THE FIGHT AGAINST CLIMATE CHANGE...

...AND **ESKOM** CUSTOMERS CAN LOOK FORWARD TO "EARTH MORNING"... "EARTH AFTERNOON"... "EARTH ENTIRE DAY"... AND "EARTH WEEK."

AND STARTING TONIGHT... "SURPRISE EARTH EVENING!" ⸨CLICK⸩

@X#X!!

CLASS, YOU HAVE 45 MINUTES TO COMPLETE THIS TEST ON GOVERN-MENT. READY? BEGIN.

"QUESTION 1: WHO IS IN CHARGE OF NATIONAL TELECOMMUNICATIONS?"

TELKOM.

"QUESTION 2: WHO IS IN CHARGE OF THE NATIONAL POWER SUPPLY?"

ESKOM.

"QUESTION 3: WHO IS IN CHARGE OF OUR **NATIONAL BROADCASTER?**"

DINA PULE'S **BOYFRIEND.**

Panel 1: AND IN OTHER NEWS... EXPELLED ANCYL PRESIDENT *JULIUS MALEMA* MAY FACE A **JAIL TERM** FOR FRAUD AND CONTEMPT OF COURT.

Panel 2: YOU **SEE?** THAT'S WHAT **HAPPENS** IN POLITICS IF YOU LIE, **CHEAT** AND **STEAL.**

Panel 3:

Panel 4: ...WHAT?

Panel 5: APPEARING BEFORE THE NATIONAL ASSEMBLY, **PRESIDENT ZUMA** WAS ASKED IF HE WAS INFORMED OF THE R 206 MILLION UPGRADE TO HIS **NKANDLA RESIDENCE.**

Panel 6: THE PRESIDENT SAID HE WAS "INFORMED", **BUT** THE **SPECIFICS** AND **COST** WERE DECIDED BY "THE RELEVANT OFFICIALS" THROUGH THEIR DEPARTMENTS.

Panel 7: WHILE THE **ANC** FELT HE ANSWERED ALL THE QUESTIONS, MANY FELT HE WAS **TAP-DANCING** AROUND THE REAL ISSUES.

Panel 8: WHO, **ME?!** HIT IT! BIG FINISH!! HE'S PRETTY LIGHT ON HIS FEET FOR A MAN HIS AGE. TAP TAP TAP TAP TAP TAP TAP TAP TAP TAP TAP TAP

Panel 9: COMING UP... "THE YOUNG AND THE RESTING."

Panel 10: FOLLOWED BY "PRACTICE-GAME OF THRONES"... "THE JUST-OKAY WIFE"...

Panel 11: "SEMI-DESPERATE HOUSEWIVES"... AND OUR POPULAR CURRENT AFFAIRS PROGRAMME, "ORDINARY ASSIGNMENT."

Panel 12: YOU'RE WATCHING THE **MEDIOCRITY CHANNEL** ...BROUGHT TO YOU BY SAA, TELKOM, ESKOM AND THE SABC.

MADAM & Eve

BY STEPHEN FRANCIS & RICO

GANGNAM STYLE SOUTH AFRICA

MADAM-NAM STYLE

GANGLAND STYLE

BLAM! BLAM!

BLAM! BLAM! BLAM! BLAM!

PARLIAMENT-NAM STYLE

ZZZZZZ ZZZZZZ ZZZZZZ

SNORE!

ZZZZ

SLAM-SLAM STYLE

SLAM!!

ATM BANG-NAM STYLE

KA-BLAM!!

ATM

©RAPID PHASE · 2013

ESKOM STYLE

G✱#✱!!

STRICTLY COME DANCING -- INTO THE CENTRAL AFRICAN REPUBLIC

Panel 1: AND IN OTHER NEWS... PARLIAMENT HAS BEEN ASKED TO **PROBE** MINISTER **PULE** OVER ALLEGED CORRUPTION.

Panel 2: ... JULIUS MALEMA IS BEING **PROBED** OVER HIS "HIDDEN ASSETS" ... AND PRESIDENT ZUMA IS FACING A **PROBE** OVER HIS **NKANDLA** EXPENDITURE...

©RAPID PHASE - 2013

Panel 3: WOW!! A LOT OF PEOPLE SEEM TO BE GETTING **PROBED** LATELY. WHAT HAPPENS THEN?

USUALLY **NOTHING.**

Panel 4: THAT'S WHY THEY CALL IT "PROBATION."

MOM!

www.madamandeve.co.za

Panel 5: AND IN OTHER NEWS... IN **ZIMBABWE**, TWO PROVINCIAL OFFICIALS WERE CHARGED WITH **STEALING CATTLE** MEANT FOR ROBERT MUGABE'S **BIRTHDAY PARTY.**

www.madamandeve.co.za

Panel 6: I WONDER HOW THEY GOT **CAUGHT?**

Panel 7: MORONS.

©RAPID PHASE-2013

Panel 8: TODAY'S TOP STORIES... MOUNTING **CRITICISM** OVER THE DEATH OF 13 SANDF SOLDIERS IN THE CENTRAL AFRICAN REPUBLIC ...

Panel 9: A LARGE PERCENTAGE OF STUDENTS **STILL** HAVE NOT RECEIVED ALL THEIR SCHOOL **TEXTBOOKS** ...

©RAPID PHASE - 2013

Panel 10: A NEW STUDY REVEALS THAT MORE THAN **HALF** OF SOUTH AFRICANS LIVE BELOW THE **POVERTY LINE** ... AND FINALLY...

Panel 11: ... **KIM KARDASHIAN** LOVES BEING **PREGNANT**, BUT CAN'T "WAIT TO **SQUEEZE** HER FAMOUS **BUTT** INTO HER **SKINNY JEANS!**

TURN IT UP!

WHAT?!

SHHH!

Panel 1: I HAVE **ONE HUNDRED** RAND! ONE HUNDRED RAND! DO I HEAR **TWO HUNDRED**?!
ONE HUNDRED AND **ONE** RAND!

Panel 2: **SOLD!!** TO THE STINGY WHITE GOGO IN THE SECOND ROW!

Panel 3:  CONGRATULATIONS. YOU JUST BOUGHT A HISTORIC COLLECTOR'S ITEM.
I DID?

Panel 4:  MOM? WHATEVER **POSSESSED** YOU TO BUY JULIUS MALEMA'S OLD **BERET**? ...MOM?
MUST... GO... TO... LIMPOPO.
TO BE CONTINUED!

Panel 5:  MADAM-- SINCE **WHEN** DOES YOUR MOTHER EAT **SUSHI**?
EVER SINCE SHE BOUGHT **MALEMA'S** OLD **BERET** AT THE AUCTION, SHE'S BEEN ACTING WEIRD.

Panel 6:  BRACE YOURSELF, MADAM! SHE COULD BE **POSSESSED**... BY THE BERET'S **JUJU VOODOO**!
...JUJU VOODOO? HOW CAN YOU <u>TELL</u>?

Panel 7:  **EVE!!** IT'S AFTER FIVE! WHERE'S MY **EXPENSIVE SINGLE MALT WHISKEY**?!

Panel 8:  UH-OH. WE MAY HAVE A PROBLEM.
JAHELA! NGILAMBILE!

Panel 9:  **EVE!** WHAT ARE WE GOING TO DO? MY MOTHER'S BEEN **POSSESSED** BY THE SPIRIT OF **MALEMA'S BERET**.

Panel 10:  **BLOODY AGENT!!**

Panel 11:  ...WHEN'S DINNER?

Panel 12:  SOMETIMES THE SIMPLEST SOLUTION IS THE MOST EFFECTIVE.
AND WHERE'S MY **GIN & TONIC**?!

THANK GOODNESS MOM'S BACK TO HER OLD SELF, AND NO LONGER POSSESSED BY JULIUS MALEMA'S OLD BERET.

EXCEPT... WHAT DID YOU DO WITH THE BERET?

I THREW IT AWAY OUTSIDE IN THE DUSTBIN. WHY?

UH-OH.

BLOODY AGENT WEEDS!!

SPRITZ! SPRITZ!

FAREWELL, MARGARET THATCHER.

SADLY, THERE WILL ONLY BE ONE "IRON LADY."

I WISH!!

LOOK... IT'S "2001, A SPACE ODDYSSEY." ¦SIGH¦...IT BRINGS BACK SUCH MEMORIES.

DA DA DA DA!

...BECAUSE IT'S ONE OF YOUR FAVOURITE FILMS?

NO, BECAUSE WE HAVEN'T PAID OUR SABC TV LICENSE SINCE THE YEAR 2001.

BE CAREFUL, MADAM. WHAT IF THE GOVERNMENT FINDS A WAY TO STOP YOU FROM WATCHING TELEVISION?

STOP ME? HA! I'D LIKE TO SEE THEM TRY!

¦CLICK¦

I REST MY CASE.

NOT FAIR! "ACTS OF ESKOM" DON'T COUNT!

MADAM & Eve
BY STEPHEN FRANCIS & RICO

THAT TRUST FUND WAS PROMISED TO ME!

GIVE ME THAT CHEQUE-BOOK!

WHAT-EVERRR!

... AND WE'LL BE BACK WITH MORE "BEING MANDELA" ... AFTER THIS.

UNBELIEVABLE! IS THERE ANYTHING THEY WON'T TURN INTO A REALITY TV SHOW THESE DAYS ?!

PROJECT ZUMA: EXTREME PRESIDENTIAL MAKEOVER

REMOVE THE NEGATIVE, ACCENTUATE THE POSITIVE... AND CREATE A NEW IMAGE: AN APPEALING, TRUSTWORTHY WORLD LEADER WITH INTEGRITY, POISE AND CONFIDENCE.

BEFORE: AFTER:

Pimp My Tender

CONGRATULATIONS, MY SON. YOU'RE BUILDING A NEW ROAD TO PRETORIA.

THE APPRENTICE BURGLAR

WHOOP! WHOOP! WHO

OOPS.

SETTING OFF THE ALARM. NICE GOING.

WHAT DID I TELL YOU ?! CUT THE RED WIRE! YOU'RE FIRED!

SIR? I THINK THE POLICE ARE HERE.

Till Ladies

JOIN PRECIOUS, LIZZIE AND ... WE FORGET THE OTHER ONE -- AS THEY SPEND A HIGH-SPIRITED DAY AT PICK 'N PAY!

CORRUPTION BUSTERS

CANCELLED AFTER ONE EPISODE - SABC

BEiNG MADAM & Eve

✓ Sleeping on ironing boards?
✓ Shooting katties at Mielie Ladies?

Madams sitting around all day drinking gin & tonics, reading newspapers and watching TV? THIS is entertaining? WHO's GOING TO WATCH A SHOW LIKE THIS?

CANCELLED!

MADAM & Eve

BY STEPHEN FRANCIS & RICO

AND IN OTHER NEWS, A **SURVEY** COMMISSIONED BY THE **ANC** SHOWS THAT MANY SUPPORTERS ARE **UNHAPPY** WITH THE CONDUCT OF THEIR LEADERS AND FEEL THEY ARE OUT OF TOUCH WITH ORDINARY PEOPLE.

REACTION WAS SWIFT AND CERTAIN FROM THE PRESIDENT.

WHAT **IDIOT** COMMISSIONED THAT **SURVEY**?!

NKANDLA

OUT OF TOUCH? RIDICULOUS!

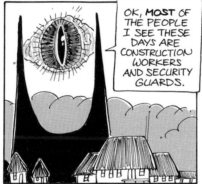

OK, **MOST** OF THE PEOPLE I SEE THESE DAYS ARE CONSTRUCTION WORKERS AND SECURITY GUARDS.

... AND FROM **KGALEMA MOTLANTHE** ON A MILLION RAND HOLIDAY IN THE SEYCHELLES?

PEOPLE WHO NEED PEOPLE ... ARE THE LUCKIEST PEOPLE IN THE WORLD.

... AND BEFORE ANYONE CRITICISES ME FOR SPENDING A **MILLION BUCKS** ON A BEACHFRONT HOLIDAY, IT'S ALL PERFECTLY **ALLOWABLE** ... ACCORDING TO THE **PRESIDENTIAL HANDBOOK.**

... EVEN THOUGH I'M NOT PRESIDENT.

THE PRESIDENTIAL HANDBOOK! WERE THE LEGENDS **TRUE**? DID IT REALLY **EXIST**?

SOME SAY...IT HAS A DARK POWER FOR CORRUPTION AND GREED.

MY PRECIOUS!   MINE!   GIVE IT TO ME!

© RAPID PHASE · 2013

THE **MANDELA** FAMILY MIGHT KNOW ... BUT THEY'RE NOT TALKING.

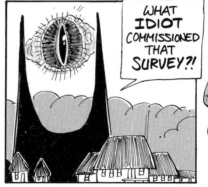

WHAT **IDIOT** COMMISSIONED THAT **SURVEY**?!

AND THEN ONE DAY... THE HANDBOOK CAUSED ITSELF TO BE FOUND BY...

HEY! LOOK!   ... A LITTLE HOBBIT.

TO BE CONTINUED?

AND IN OTHER NEWS... **IDENTITY THEFT** HAS BECOME THE NATION'S NUMBER ONE **WHITE COLLAR CRIME**...

AAAAAH!!

I DON'T THINK THAT'S EXACTLY WHAT THEY MEAN BY "IDENTITY THEFT."

I COUNT 39 VISIBLE NOSE HAIRS.

CHECK.

HUH...? **WHAT** ARE YOU STARING AT?

FRANKLY, WE'RE CONCERNED. THE NEWS SAID THAT "**IDENTITY THEFT**" IS ON THE RISE. HOW CAN WE BE **SURE** YOU ARE WHO YOU **SAY** YOU ARE?

SLAM!!

WELL... **THAT** WAS A GOOD SIGN.

BUT STILL **NOT** CONCLUSIVE.

UNREASONABLY GROUCHY.

CHECK.

STILL CHASING MIELIE LADY WITH KATTY?

CHECK.

ALWAYS WEARS PURPLE... AND HAS HAIR-TRIGGER TEMPER ISSUES?

CHECK.

EXCESSIVE CONSUMPTION OF GIN & TONIC.

CHECK.

GREAT NEWS. AFTER CAREFUL CONSIDERATION, WE'VE DECIDED YOU'RE **NOT** A VICTIM OF "IDENTITY THEFT"... AND ARE, IN FACT, **YOU**.

SLAM!!

SOME PEOPLE JUST HATE HEARING **GOOD NEWS**.

WHOA! **MANDELAS!** WAIT! WE HAVEN'T EVEN **BEGUN** YET!

PUNCH!
BIFF!
POW!

WHO WANTS TO BE A **MILLIONAIRE...?** AND HOW BADLY DO YOU **WANT** TO? WE'LL FIND OUT SOON, BECAUSE IT'S TIME TO PLAY SA'S NEWEST GAME SHOW...

LONG WALK TO FREEDOM, SHORT WALK TO THE BANK!!

COMING UP FIRST: OUR LIGHTNING KICKBOXING ROUND!

FINALLY SOMETHING GOOD ON SABC.

©RAPID PHASE 2013

BOB's HOUSE OF HANDBOOKS

PRESIDENTIAL HANDBOOKS!

MINISTERIAL HANDBOOKS!

TENDERPRENEURIAL HANDBOOKS!

OPEN

IF IT REALLY EXISTED, WE'VE **GOT** IT!

SALE!!

ANCYL HANDBOOKS!

DOMESTIC HANDBOOKS!

MADAM HANDBOOKS!

© RAPID PHASE - 2013

THANDI, WHERE'S YOUR HOMEWORK?

MY DOG ATE IT.

BUT IT'S OKAY. ACCORDING TO THE "**STUDENTARIAL HANDBOOK**"... EACH PUPIL IS ALLOWED **FIVE SUSPICIOUS EXCUSES** FOR HOMEWORK NON-COMPLIANCE BEFORE PUNITIVE ACTION MAY BE TAKEN.

HEY, IT WAS WORTH A SHOT.

PRINCIPAL

MADAM & Eve BY STEPHEN FRANCIS & RICO

AND IN OTHER NEWS, PRESIDENT ZUMA HAS BEEN SEVERELY CRITICISED FOR TAKING ADVANTAGE OF A FRAIL **NELSON MANDELA** FOR THE BENEFIT OF TV CAMERAS AND PHOTOGRAPHERS.

MADIBA! YOU'RE LOOKING GREAT!

COME CLOSER...

YOUR SUIT IS VERY UGLY.

MADIBA SAYS HE'S **THRILLED** WE'RE ALL HERE!

I PUT A SAUSAGE ROLL WHERE YOU'RE SITTING.

HE SAYS VIVA, ANC VIVA! ...AND FEELS **FINE!**

SMILE, TATA!

I'D RATHER JOIN THE D.A.!

HE SAYS HE'S **READY!** LET'S TAKE SOME **PHOTOS!**

©RAPID PHASE – 2013

CLICK! CLICK! CLICK! CLICK! CLICK! CLICK! CLICK! CLICK! CLICK! CLICK! CLICK!

THAT'S ODD. WHY IS HE SMILING **NOW?**

AND IN OTHER NEWS, **ESKOM** HAS WARNED CONSUMERS TO EXPECT MANY **BLACKOUTS** THIS WINTER.

© RAPID PHASE - 2013
www.madamandeve.co.za

THE **ESKOM** BOARD SAY THEY'RE NOT **WORRIED**, BECAUSE ACCORDING TO THE SOUTH AFRICAN **ELECTRICITY HANDBOOK**...

AAAAH!

ROLLING ESKOM BLACK-OUT?

YOUR MOTHER **BLEW** THE CIRCUIT BREAKER.

THREE GREEN **R1000** BOTTLES OF **WHISKEY** HANGING ON THE WALL...

... AND IF ONE GREEN **R1000** BOTTLE OF **WHISKEY** SHOULD ACCIDENTALLY FALL...

... THERE'LL BE **TWO** GREEN R1000 BOTTLES OF WHISKEY HANGING ON THE WALL...

HEY -- LOOK WHAT I **FOUND** UNDER THE SEAT!

www.madamandeve.co.za

I SAY, OLD CHAP! SOMEBODY CALL THE **COPS**! HOO-HOO!

TEN-FOUR! COPY THAT! HA-HA-HA!

© RAPID PHASE - 2013

AND IN OTHER NEWS, **THIEVES** BROKE INTO FORMER POLICE COMMISSIONER **BHEKI CELE'S** GARAGE AND STOLE THREE BOTTLES OF WHISKEY FROM HIS CAR.

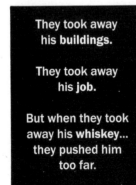

They took away his **buildings**.

They took away his **job**.

But when they took away his **whiskey**... they pushed him too far.

ASK YOURSELF... "DID I DRINK **TWO** BOTTLES... OR ONLY **ONE**? DO I FEEL LUCKY?" WELL **DO** YOU, PUNK?!

... AND WHILE YOU'RE AT IT, HAND BACK MY **HATS**, TOO.

© RAPID PHASE - 2013

ONE MAN SINGLE MALT SINGLE-MINDED

GO AHEAD, MAKE MINE A DOUBLE.

DIRTY BHEKI

Coming soon!

BAD NEWS. THE **TRIBE** HAS VOTED YOU **OUT**.

OH YEAH? WELL, **MY** TRIBE HAS VOTED ME **IN**!

... BUT I WAS GOING TO **LEAVE** ANYWAY.

NO, YOU'RE NOT.

YES, I AM!

I'M CALLING THE PUBLIC PROTECTOR!

AND WE'LL BE BACK... WITH MORE OF **SABC BOARD SURVIVOR** ... AFTER **THIS**.

FINALLY, A DECENT REALITY SHOW.

TODAY'S TOP STORY... THE SOUTH AFRICAN POLICE SERVICE HAS RELEASED THIS YEAR'S **CRIME STATISTICS**, ADMITTING THAT HOUSE-BREAKING AND BURGLARY ARE ON THE RISE.

@#✳#!!

AND THIS JUST IN... POLICE ARE INVESTIGATING THE THEFT OF **MILLIONS STOLEN** FROM THE SOLD OUT **JUSTIN BIEBER** CONCERT THIS WEEKEND.

YAY!!

WHAT?

AND I WAS LIKE- BABY, BABY, BABY--OOH! ♪

LIKE- BABY, BABY, BABY NOOO! ♪

LIKE BABY, ♪ BABY, BABY-OOH! ♪

DO YOU **MIND?** I'M TRYING TO **WORK** HERE.

SORRY.

97

MADAM & Eve
BY STEPHEN FRANCIS & RICO

GUPTAGATE
Memorial Merchandise

GUP a SOUP — WHEN YOU'RE REALLY IN THE THICK OF IT!

I survived Guptagate and all I got was a lousy exoneration!

BOTTLED WATERKLOOF — SPARKLING OR PLANE WATER. Comes at a very high price. **WK**

ASSORTED NUPTIAL GUPCAKES — CELEBRATE THE GUPTA WEDDING EVERY DAY! INCREDIBLY RICH! IMPORTED DIRECT FROM INDIA!

GUPZILLA — UNSTOPPABLE! UNMANAGEABLE! UNCONTROLLABLE!

THE NEW GUPTA CORRUPTA — GO ANYWHERE YOU WANT! DO ANYTHING YOU WANT!

©RAPID PHASE - 2013

GUPTAMAN — CAN FLY ANYWHERE AT A MOMENT'S NOTICE! MORE POWERFUL THAN SHAIKMAN! NO LANDING RIGHTS NECESSARY!

LEGO GUPTAGATE WEDDING SET — INCLUDES BRIDE, GROOM, GUESTS AND EMBARRASSED MINISTERS. AIRPLANE AND WATERKLOOF AIRPORT SETS SOLD SEPARATELY!

HAVE YOU HEARD, MR PRESIDENT? THE **GUPTA BROTHERS** BOOKED A **PRIVATE** SHOWING OF THE **CIRQUE DU SOLEIL** AS A WEDDING PRESENT.

SO? WHO **CARES?** AS LONG AS IT DOESN'T **EMBARRASS** ME.

WELL, SIR... NOW THAT YOU MENTION IT.

INSPIRED BY TRUE EVENTS.

SIR-- ZIMBABWE HAS JUST DECLARED **WAR** ON US!

WHAT?! **SCRAMBLE OUR FIGHTERS!**

NO CAN DO, SIR! THERE'S A PLANE FULL OF TWO HUNDRED CIVILIAN **WEDDING GUESTS** IN THE MIDDLE OF THE **RUNWAY!**

WHAT?!

WELL, SUIT 'EM UP, GIVE THEM EACH A **RIFLE** AND SEND 'EM **IN!** THIS IS A MATTER OF **NATIONAL SECURITY!**

YES, SIR!

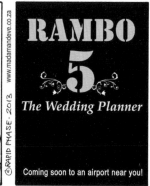

RAMBO 5

The Wedding Planner

Coming soon to an airport near you!

AND IN MORE **GUPTAGATE** NEWS, SOURCES SAY THAT THE **GUPTA** PROBE INTO THE **GUPTA** JET LANDING IS A POLITICAL HOT POTATO ...

...WE'LL BE BACK WITH MORE **GUPTA** NEWS IN JUST A MINUTE ...

≈SIGH≈ **GUPTA THIS. GUPTA THAT. GUPTA! GUPTA! GUPTA!**

AWK! GUPTA! GUPTA!

GUPTA! GUPTA!

GUPTA! GUPTA! GUPTA! GUPTA!

"COMMUNITY CHEST: BOMB SQUAD BLOWS UP YOUR **WEDDING INVITATION**, LOSE ONE TURN." DARN.

THREE! ONE, TWO, THREE. "GET OUT OF JAIL AS MUCH AS YOU WANT" CARD.

SIGH

TWO. ONE, TWO! MINISTRY OF DEFENCE! **BUY** IT!

YOU ALREADY **OWN** IT.

OH.

GUPTA BROTHERS MONOPOLY.

TODAY'S TOP STORY: A PRELIMINARY REPORT ON THE **GUPTAGATE** SCANDAL **EXONERATES** PRESIDENT ZUMA, ALL GOVERNMENT OFFICIALS AND ALL MEMBERS OF THE GUPTA FAMILY.

INSTEAD, **BLAME** FOR THE ILLEGAL LANDING IS ATTRIBUTED TO **ONE** MAN: DUMISANE NYONI, AIRPORT RUNWAY CONTROLLER.

IN THIS EXCLUSIVE FOOTAGE, DUMISANE NOT ONLY **ALLOWS** THE PLANE TO **LAND**, BUT ALLEGEDLY **HELPS** THE PASSENGERS **DISEMBARK**.

DUMISANE CLAIMS HE'S "INNOCENT" AND HE WAS **UNAWARE** HE WAS COMMITTING HIGH TREASON AND WAS JUST -QUOTE- "DOING HIS JOB."

GWEN!!

HOOT IF YOU KNOW THE GUPTAS!

www.madamandeve.co.za © RAPID PHASE - 2013

AND THIS JUST IN: THE RELEASE OF THE OFFICIAL REPORT ON "GUPTAGATE" INDICATES THAT THERE WAS INDEED "PRESSURE FROM **NUMBER ONE** TO ALLOW THE PLANE TO LAND..."

"...ALTHOUGH THERE IS **NO CONCLUSIVE PROOF** THAT "NUMBER ONE" REFERS TO **PRESIDENT ZUMA.**

WHAT?!

WHAT A LOAD OF NUMBER **TWO!**

IS NUMBER ONE IN?

WHO WANTS TO KNOW?

NUMBER FOUR. I'M HERE WITH **NUMBER FIVE.**

MISTER PRESIDENT? ...NUMBERS FOUR AND FIVE ARE HERE FOR THE MEETING.

HE SAYS "WHAT ABOUT NUMBER **TWO** AND NUMBER **THREE?**

THEY'RE RUNNING LATE. SO **MISTER X** IS FILLING IN FOR THEM.

SO **X** EQUALS **4 + 5** MINUS **2 + 3.** GOOD. SEND THEM ALL IN.

I'LL REALLY BE GLAD WHEN WE CAN USE OUR OWN NAMES AGAIN.

BAD NEWS, MISTER PRESIDENT. THE **GUPTAS** WANT THE TITLE OF "**NUMBER ONE.**"

WHAT?! BUT **I'M** NUMBER ONE, DAMMIT!

SHH. DON'T SAY THAT OUT LOUD, SIR. IT CASTS A **BAD LIGHT** ON OUR REPORT.

≷SIGH≷ BUT HOW CAN ALL **THREE** GUPTAS BE **NUMBER ONE?**

"NUMBER 1a)" "NUMBER 1b)" AND "NUMBER 1c)".

AND WHAT ABOUT **ME?!** WHO AM I NOW?!

THEY SUGGEST EITHER "**LORD MUCKY-MUCK**" OR "**GRAND POOBAH.**" PICK ONE.

I HATE BIG WEDDINGS.

"THE BOSS!" WHAT DO YOU THINK, SIR?

NOT BAD...

...BUT ISN'T THAT WHAT THEY CALL **BRUCE SPRINGSTEEN?**

YES. WELL SPOTTED, MISTER PRESIDENT.

WHAT ABOUT..."THE CHAIRMAN OF THE BOARD?"

TOO FRANK SINATRA.

"THE LEADER OF THE PACK?"

TOO PHIL SPECTOR.

"THE GODFATHER?"

...OF SOUL? JAMES BROWN? **FORGET** IT.

WHAT ABOUT "THE BIG CHEESE?"

TOO MACDONALDS.

"THE MAN WITH NO NAME?"

TOO CLINT EASTWOOD.

"THE HEAD HONCHO."

NO.

"TOP DOG?"

NOPE.

"THE BIG KAHUNA?"

NEGATIVE.

"LORD MUCKY MUCK?"

NO!

"THE GRAND POOBAH!"

YOU MUST BE **JOKING.**

≧ SIGH ≦

...WHY CAN'T I **STILL** BE **NUMBER ONE?**

IT'S BEEN COMPROMISED, MR PRESIDENT. YOU <u>KNOW</u> THAT.

...AND ANYWAY, THE **GUPTAS** HAVE ALREADY PUT A DEPOSIT ON "NUMBER ONE", THE **NEXT** TIME IT BECOMES **AVAILABLE.**

G#☆#G!!

WAIT! I'VE GOT IT! CALL ME..."NUMERO UNO!"

PLEASE, SIR. TRY AND FOCUS.

WHAT'S THAT, MADAM?

THE **OWNER'S MANUAL** FOR THE TELEVISION.

I'M TRYING TO FIGURE OUT HOW TO SET THE **PARENTAL CONTROL.**

...TO BLOCK **X-RATED** MOVIES?

AAARGH!! UNBELIEVABLE!! ©#☆#©!!!

THUD!!

...TO BLOCK THE **MORNING NEWS HEADLINES.**

www.madamandeve.co.za
© RAPID PHASE - 2013

WE'RE STUDYING THE **BIG BANG THEORY** IN SCHOOL.

WHAT DO **YOU** KNOW ABOUT THE **BIG BANG?**

BANG!!

www.madamandeve.co.za
© RAPID PHASE - 2013

AND THEY WONDER WHY OUR EDUCATION SYSTEM IS IN SO MUCH TROUBLE.

THE WALKING DEAD, SOUTH AFRICA

BRAAAINS! BRAAAAINS! BRRAAAINS!

OH, NO! ZOMBIES! RUN!!

LOOK! THE POLICE! WE'RE SAVED!!

© RAPID PHASE - 2013

BRRIIIBES! BRIIIIBES! BRRIIIBES!

MOM-- WHAT ARE YOU DOING WITH THAT **BALACLAVA**?

AN EXPERIMENT. WE **TIP** THAT CAR GUARD A FORTUNE TO WATCH THE CAR. I WANT TO SEE WHAT HE'LL **DO** IN A REAL **EMERGENCY**.

-SQUEAK-

-CLANK!-

COME...COME...COME... WAIT! OK, COME...COME...

HEY! I JUST **REALISED**! ...THERE'S "**ADAM & EVE**" ...AND YOU GUYS ARE **MADAM & EVE**!

THERE'S **LOTS** OF SIMILARITIES! **THEY** LIVED IN THE **GARDEN OF EDEN** AND **YOU** STAY IN AN **ENCLOSED** NEIGHBOURHOOD WITH A GARDENER.

THEY HAD TO DEAL WITH A TEDIOUS **SERPENT**... AND **YOU** HAVE TO DEAL WITH --

SLAM!!

WELL, THAT'S THE END OF THAT **METAPHOR**!

HEY! WE'VE BEEN **CAST OUT!!**

OUR ENGLISH TEACHER IS SO **SICK**, IT'S UNBELIEVABLE.

THEN STAY AWAY FROM SCHOOL.

WHY? WE WANT TO BE **SICK**, TOO!

APPARENTLY... THERE SEEMS TO BE A COMMUNICATION PROBLEM. IN THIS CASE "**SICK**"... MEANS "TOTALLY **COOL**."

NEVER MIND. FORGET THE WHOLE THING. HOW'S **CHEMISTRY** CLASS?

IT'S THE **BOMB**!

SOME PEOPLE CAN'T **HANDLE** A SIMPLE OPINION.

SPRING

SUMMER

AUTUMN

WINTER

WELCOME TO OUR **CALL CENTRE HELPLINE.** THANK YOU FOR HOLDING. ALL OUR CONSULTANTS ARE STILL BUSY. WE VALUE...

© RAPID PHASE - 2013

www.madamandeve.co.za

LOOK--THERE'S THAT **DOG** AGAIN. SNEAKING IN TO WATCH TV!

WAIT-- HOW DOES HE **DO** IT? HOW DOES HE GET PAST OUR **SECURITY**, WALLS AND GATES? KEEP AN **EYE** ON HIM!

©RAPID PHASE - 2013

I WONDER IF BLOCKWATCH KNOWS ABOUT THIS?

www.madamandeve.co.za

AND IN OTHER NEWS, A COMMUTER ADVISORY WARNS OF THE POSSIBILITY OF SEVERAL DISRUPTIVE **WILDCAT STRIKES** TOMORROW MORNING.

MAYBE YOU SHOULD TAKE A DIFFERENT ROUTE TO SCHOOL.

ON STRIKE!

WILDCAT UNION

©RAPID PHASE - 2013

FORGET **THAT.** I'M CALLING IN **SICK.**

AND WE'LL BE BACK... WITH MORE UPDATES ON FORMER PRESIDENT **NELSON MANDELA'S** CONDITION... AFTER THIS.

www.madamandeve.co.za

©RAPID PHASE - 2013

AND NOW, JUSTICE MINISTER RADEBE WILL READ THE "NAME AND SHAME" **LIST** OF **GOVERNMENT OFFICIALS** GUILTY OF **CORRUPTION.**

RING-RING

HELLO? NO, YOU'RE NOT ON THE LIST. YOU'RE WELCOME.

RING RING

RING RING

NO, YOU'RE NOT ON.

NO, YOU'RE NOT ON.

RING RING!

RING RING

NOPE. NOT YOU.

RING RING!

NO, NO. NOT YOU.

www.madamandeve.co.za

©RAPID PHASE - 2013

MISTER PRESIDENT-- ALL OUR **PHONE** LINES ARE **DOWN** AND ALL OF **PARLIAMENT** IS AT A **STANDSTILL.**

NEVER MIND **THAT!** DID HE GET TO THE **"Z 's"** YET?

AND IN OTHER NEWS, **JULIUS MALEMA** WANTS TO START A NEW **PARTY.**

DID YOU HEAR, GWEN? **JULIUS MALEMA** WANTS TO START A NEW **PARTY.**

HMM.

IT'S A FREE COUNTRY.

www.madamandeve.co.za

©RAPID PHASE - 2013

BUT IF HE DOESN'T KEEP THE **NOISE** DOWN AFTER **MIDNIGHT**, I'M CALLING THE COPS TO **COMPLAIN.**

MADAM & Eve

BY STEPHEN FRANCIS & RICO

AND IN OTHER NEWS... JULIUS MALEMA WANTS TO START A NEW POLITICAL PARTY CALLED THE "ECONOMIC FREEDOM FIGHTERS."

ANOTHER PARTY? I THOUGHT HE WAS BROKE.

FINALLY! -- "SURE-FIRE POLITICAL PARTY MONEYSAVERS -- FOR A PARTY EVERYONE CAN AFFORD." ... EVEN ME!

CATALOGUE

THINGS TO GET: **BUDGET BODYGUARDS**

BOB's BUDGET BODYGUARDS

BANG!

LOW-BUDGET BLUE LIGHT BRIGADE

EFF

PUTTPUTTPUTTPUTTP

ECONOMY-SIZE INFLATABLE **ENTOURAGE**

PFFT! PFFT! PFFT!

MONEY-SAVING RECYCLED POLITICAL T-SHIRTS

WE WILL KILL ~~FOR~~ ZUMA

PLATFORM CATCHPHRASE:

EFF
SAVE ME THE MONEY!

© RAPID PHASE - 2013

SINGLE MALT WHISKEY BALLS

BUDGET THEME SONG

BRING ME MY MACHINE GUN FROM THE PAWN SHOP...

PAWN

BUDGET-FRIENDLY PARTY FOOD

EATING McNUGGETS OFF OF RONALD McDONALD

Panel 1:
(AHEM) "THERE'S A TOKOLOSHE IN MY LUNCH BOX."

Panel 2:
"IT WAS AN ORDINARY SCHOOL DAY WHEN (NAME WITHHELD) SAT DOWN WITH FRIENDS FOR LUNCH."

Panel 3:

"SUDDENLY (NAME WITHHELD) HEARD A SOFT VOICE COMING FROM HIS LUNCH BOX: "HELP! LET ME OUT!"

Panel 4:

I THOUGHT WE WERE SUPPOSED TO DO A REPORT ON TOPICAL HEADLINES!

PRINCIPAL

Panel 5:

QUESTION # 1: JULIUS MALEMA SAID "SOUTH AFRICA COULD BECOME A KLEPTOCRACY -- A GOVERNMENT RULED BY GREED." CAN YOU NAME TWO OTHER TYPES OF GOVERNMENT?

Panel 6:

A "STIR FRY IN A WOKRACY" -- A GOVERNMENT BASED ON ASIAN EATING HABITS!

Panel 7:

"CAPTAIN KIRK AND SPOCKRACY" --GOVERNMENT OFFICIALS STAY HOME ALL DAY, WATCHING OLD STAR TREK RERUNS.

Panel 8:

HEY! MINE SOUNDED JUST AS GOOD AS HIS DID!

PRINCIPAL

Panel 9:

WHAT ARE YOU DOING?

BECOMING A ZILLIONAIRE LIKE THE GUY WHO THOUGHT UP THE TEENAGE MUTANT NINJA TURTLES!

Panel 10:

I'VE PROGRAMMED YOUR LAPTOP TO SPIT OUT SIMILAR YET ARBITRARY DESCRIPTIVE ANIMAL GROUPS! THEN I DRAW THEM UP AND WAIT FOR THE MONEY TO ROLL IN. IT'S FOOLPROOF!

Panel 11:

ADOLESCENT KICKBOXING SPECKLED SEA URCHINS

Panel 12:

...MONEY ROLLING IN, YET?

NO. I NEED A PUBLICITY STUNT. CAN YOU RIDE A MOTORCYCLE?

SYSTEM ERROR

The punchline you were looking for is not available.

The file is missing or corrupt. Try restarting the cartoon strip or contact your media service provider.

Chicken Little

THE RAND IS FALLING! THE RAND IS FALLING!

HEY-- THAT'S **NOT** HOW I REMEMBER THIS STORY.

IT'S THE ECONOMIC **RECESSION** EDITION.

MOM!!

FALLING ROCKS ZONE

FALLING RAND ZONE

OKAY, **HERE!** ONE FOR **YOU**... AND ONE FOR **YOU.**

...**HAPPY** NOW?

HAVE A NICE DAY. LET'S GO, GWEN.

VROOM!!

I DON'T THINK THAT'S WHAT THEY **MEANT** BY "BUY US A **COOLDRINK**."

JUST KEEP DRIVING.

"POLITICAL WITCH HUNT"

"ANC CHIEF WHIP"

"AUNTY-CORRUPTION"

ARE YOU **POSITIVE** YOU READ THE "INTRODUCTION TO GOVERNMENT" TEXTBOOK?

SURE. WHY DO YOU ASK?

OH, GOOD. **DETECTIVE NOVELS** FOR YOUNG READERS -- **I** USED TO READ THEM WHEN I WAS **YOUR** AGE.

"**THE HARDY BOYS** AND THE TAXPAYER TOWER TREASURE?"

"**NANCY DREW** AND THE SECRET OF THE ILLEGAL TENDERS?"

"**THE FAMOUS FIVE** AND THE CLUE OF THE MYSTERY AIRPLANE WEDDING GUESTS?!"

THEY'RE UPDATED 2013 **SOUTH AFRICAN** EDITIONS.

YAY! STORY TIME!

AND MOM -- STICK TO THE **STORY!** NO EMBELLISHING OR **UPDATING!**

WHICH STORY IS IT?

"LIFE IS LIKE A BOX OF CHOCOLATES. YOU NEVER **KNOW** WHAT YOU'RE GOING TO **GET.**

UNLESS YOU SLIP THE CHOCOLATIER TWENTY BUCKS!

OH BOY! "FORREST GUPTA!!"

MOM!

MADAM & Eve

BY STEPHEN FRANCIS & RICO

HOW DO YOU LIKE MY NEW **DESIGNER OUTFIT?**

IT'S...UH, VERY STYLISH, SIR.

≤GASP≥ HE'S **NOT** WEARING ANY CLOTHES. **TELL HIM!**

YOU TELL HIM!

"AND SO, NOBODY DARED TO SAY OUT LOUD WHAT EVERYONE COULD PLAINLY **SEE.**"

WHAT WERE THEY AFRAID OF? **REPERCUSSIONS?**

WORSE. **REDEPLOYMENT.**

"THIS WENT ON FOR A LONG TIME UNTIL..."

HERE COMES MY **FAVOURITE** PART!

"A BRAVE LITTLE **GIRL** SHOUTED..."

"HEY! THE EMPEROR HAS **NO CLOTHES!**"

NO, SHE SHOUTED: "THE EMPEROR HAS A 300 MILLION RAND **PALACE** BUILT WITH **TAXPAYER'S MONEY!**"

©RAPID PHASE · 2013

HEY! WHAT ABOUT THE FACT THAT HE WAS **BUTT-NAKED?!**

NOBODY CARED.

...THEY ALREADY SAW THE OIL PAINTING ANYWAY.

MOM!!

I LIKE THE OLD VERSION. WHAT'S NEXT?

"THE WHITE BOY WHO CRIED RACE CARD."

MOM!!

THIS JUST IN. NELSON MANDELA'S CONDITION IS IMPROVING.

THIS JUST IN. NELSON MANDELA'S CONDITION IS SERIOUS.

THIS JUST IN. NELSON MANDELA IS GETTING BETTER.

THIS JUST IN. NELSON MANDELA'S CONDITION IS CRITICAL, BUT STABLE.

MOM -- LOOK AT THIS! THEY'RE LAUNCHING **ANOTHER** POLITICAL PARTY!

YES. AGANG.

I KNEW THESE **"GANGS"** ARE **POWERFUL** ... BUT FORMING A THEIR OWN **PARTY?!**

NOT "A GANG," ... **AGANG!**

A **GANG!** THAT'S WHAT I **SAID!** ... EVEN **MALEMA'S** FORMING HIS <u>OWN</u> PARTY!

... I CAN'T **COPE** ANY MORE!

DON'T EVEN.

AND IN OTHER NEWS, THE **ANC** HEAD OF NATIONAL ELECTIONS SAID THAT "EVEN **FISH** AND **ANIMALS** WOULD **VOTE ANC** IF THEY COULD."

NOT SO FAST, BRU.

WHAT ABOUT **NKANDLA?**

SEEMS LIKE A **GRAVY TRAIN** TO ME.

...AND THEY'RE NOT SERIOUS ABOUT FIGHTING **RHINO POACHING.**

THEY'RE ALL FEEDING FROM THE SAME **TROUGH.**

Panel 1: TODAY'S TOP STORY... JULIUS MALEMA SAYS HE'S "SORRY" FOR GETTING JACOB ZUMA ELECTED AS PRESIDENT.

Panel 2: ...HE **ALSO** SAYS HE'S **SORRY** FOR THE THINGS HE **SAID** TO HELEN ZILLE.

Panel 3: ...NOT TO MENTION, BEING **SORRY** FOR **WEARING** THAT GOOFY **BERET**.

WHAT'S HE **DOING?!**

Panel 4:

JOIN Julius Malema's **THE APOLOGY PARTY**

Together, we can apologise more!

Panel 5: ...AND I'M SORRY FOR SINGING "KILL THE YOU-KNOW-WHO."

Panel 6: AND I'M SORRY FOR KICKING OUT THAT REPORTER...

MALEMA'S **STILL** SAYING SORRY?

Panel 7: ...AND I'M SORRY FOR CALLING HIM A "BLOODY AGENT."

YEP. GOING ON 15 MINUTES NOW.

Panel 8: AND...

DID HE APOLOGISE FOR THE GOOFY **BERET**?

TWICE.

Panel 9: "...AND I'M ALSO SORRY FOR SAYING HELEN ZILLE CAN'T **DANCE**...

MALEMA **STILL** APOLOGISING?

Panel 10: ...AND FOR CALLING DA MEMBERS **TEA LADIES** AND **GARDEN BOYS**...

BEEN GOING ON ALL **WEEKEND**.

Panel 11: ...AND I'M SORRY FOR **MISPLACING** ALL THOSE SCHOOL **TEXTBOOKS** FOR LIMPOPO...

Panel 12: ...OOPS. FORGET I **SAID** THAT.

I **KNEW** IT!!

MADAM & Eve

BY STEPHEN FRANCIS & RICO

TODAY'S TOP STORY-- **JULIUS MALEMA** SAYS HE'S **SORRY** FOR GETTING **JACOB ZUMA** ELECTED AS OUR PRESIDENT.

BUT WAIT... THERE'S **MORE!**

HE'S ALSO SORRY FOR SAYING ALL THOSE THINGS ABOUT **HELEN ZILLE.**

...AND SORRY FOR CALLING D.A. MEMBERS "TEA LADIES" AND "GARDEN BOYS."

HE'S SORRY FOR SUPPORTING **NATIONALISATION** ...AND ROBERT MUGABE.

...AND **REALLY** SORRY HE SAID HE'D "**KILL FOR ZUMA.**"

HE SAYS HE'S SORRY FOR THOSE "NEXT MORNING, BREAKFAST AND TAXI FARE" REMARKS...

HE'S SORRY FOR LIMPOPO, TENDERS FOR PALS,...AND SORRY FOR BUILDING THE UNFINISHED LUXURY HOUSE IN SANDTON.

©RAPID PHASE - 2013

HE'S SORRY FOR ALL THE SINGLE MALT WHISKEY AND WEARING THAT GOOFY BLACK **BERET**...

WHAT THE HELL **IS** THIS?!

HE'S SORRY FOR CHEATING ON HIS **TAXES**...

DO YOU WANT ME TO CHANGE THE CHANNEL? IT SAYS HERE IT'S A **TWO HOUR** SPECIAL...

HOW'S MADIBA DOING?

NO CHANGE. HE'S **AILING** BUT FAR FROM DEATH WITH A STRONG **WILL** TO **LIVE**. I'LL TELL HIS RELATIVES.

THIS JUST IN...THEY'RE TELLING MANDELA'S RELATIVES HE'S **AILING**, BUT CHANGING DEATH. HE HAS A STRONG WILL TO LIVE AND MUST FIGHT.

IN THIS EXCLUSIVE REPORT, AILING MANDELA WILL **CHANGE** DEATH. RELATIVES MUST BE **STRONG** AND **FIGHT**!

©RAPID PHASE-2013

CITY NEWS

MADIBA CHANGES WILL! RELATIVES DRINK STRONG ALE AND FIGHT TO THE DEATH!

ONCE I PUT MY SECRET PLAN INTO ACTION, OUR **FAMILY DYNASTY** WILL BE CONTROLLED BY... **ME!!**

YOU -- YOU'RE **EVIL!** YOU'LL NEVER GET **AWAY** WITH IT! WE WON'T **LET** YOU!

JUST TRY AND **STOP** ME! BWAHAHA!!

"ALL MY CHILDREN?" MANDELA FAMILY SQUABBLING.

www.madamandeve.co.za

©RAPID PHASE-2013

≧YAWN.≦

≧COUGH. COUGH.≦

≧GRUNT.≦

≧SNORE!≦

©RAPID PHASE-2013

HUH? A BUNCH OF **BORED**-LOOKING PEOPLE SITTING AROUND **TALKING, WHISPERING** AND **SLEEPING!** WHAT KIND OF TV SHOW **IS** THIS?!!

www.madamandeve.co.za

AND WE'LL BE BACK... WITH **MORE** OF THE **PARLIAMENTARY CHANNEL**... AFTER _THIS_.

AND HERE WE GO... DOWN AND DIRTY.

OOH! TWO KINGS! ONE ACE...

TWO JACKS AND ONE QUEEN! MAKE THAT **TWO** QUEENS!

WHAT'S HE DOING? PLAYING CARDS?

CABINET RESHUFFLE.

UH-OH. A COUPLE OF JOKERS.

MISTER PRESIDENT... YOUR **FOURTH** CABINET RESHUFFLE IS CAUSING QUITE A **STIR**.

SO?! I DON'T HAVE TO **EXPLAIN** MYSELF TO **ANYBODY!**

I CAN DO **WHATEVER** I WANT, **WHEN** I WANT... AND NO ONE CAN **STOP** ME!

IN FACT, I HEREBY **PROCLAIM** FROM NOW ON THAT JULY 8th IS "CABINET RESHUFFLE DAY!"

IS HE LOSING IT, OR WHAT?

I AM **UBER ZUMA!!** — THE **GREAT** AND **POWERFUL! MASTER** OF THE **UNIVERSE** AND ALL I SURVEY!

BWAHAHAHA!!

UH-OH.

GWEN!

AND IN OTHER NEWS, A NEW REPORT INDICATES THAT **TAXPAYERS** HAVE SPENT OVER **ONE MILLION** RAND ON **SECURITY** FOR THE PRESIDENT'S HERD OF PAMPERED **CATTLE.**

I LOVE THIS COUNTRY, BUT THE **CRIME**...

YES!! THE GOVERNMENT SHOULD **DO** SOMETHING!

I DON'T KNOW ABOUT **YOU** ...BUT **I** SLEEP WELL AT NIGHT.

I HEARD THERE WAS ANOTHER **KRAAL INVASION** DOWN THE ROAD!

MOO-HOO! STOP COMPLAINING!

OH BOY! CREAMED SPINACH AND GRASS SOUP AGAIN!

MADAM & Eve

BY STEPHEN FRANCIS & RICO

AND IN OTHER NEWS... **PRESIDENT ZUMA** IS **RESHUFFLING** HIS **CABINET** YET AGAIN, SAYING HE'S DOING IT **"HIS WAY"** AND **"DOESN'T** HAVE TO **EXPLAIN** ANYTHING TO **ANYONE."**

"HIS WAY?"

MISTER PRESIDENT!

MISTER PRESIDENT!

I HAVE A PREPARED STATEMENT: A **LETTER** THAT I'VE SENT TO VARIOUS **MINISTERS** -- AND THEY KNOW WHO THEY <u>ARE</u>.

≤AHEM≥ "TO WHOM IT MAY CONCERN: AND **NOW**, THE END IS **NEAR**. AND SO YOU **FACE** THE FINAL **CURTAIN.**"

"COMRADE -- I'LL SAY IT CLEAR. I'LL STATE MY CASE, OF WHICH I'M **CERTAIN.**"

"I LET YOU **RULE** YOUR **POST** TOO LONG AND NOW IT'S **TIME** TO HIT THE **HIGHWAY.**"

"SO PLEASE DON'T **CRY** BUT THAT IS **WHY**... I'M DOING THIS **MY WAY!**"

"YES, THERE WERE TIMES, THAT WE ALL **KNEW** YOU BIT OFF MORE THAN YOU COULD **CHEW.**"

"WE ALL WERE **BOUGHT** 'CEPT YOU GOT **CAUGHT.** YOU ONCE WERE **LOYAL** NOW YOU'RE MY **FOIL.**"

"YOU GAVE FRIENDS **JOBS.** YOUR BUDGET **ROBBED** YOU CAN'T SAY 'NO' YOU GOTTA **GO.**"

©RAPID PHASE-2013

"I GET NO **JOY** CAN'T **REDEPLOY...** I DID THIS **MYYYYY WAY!!**"

Signed: PRESIDENT ZUMA"

"...P.S. YOU'RE FIRED."

THIS COUNTRY GETS MORE INTERESTING EVERY DAY.

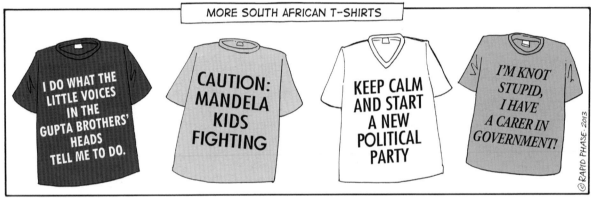

MADAM... HAVE YOU HEARD? THEY JUST ANNOUNCED THE **BIRTH** OF A **BABY BOY** TO BRITAIN'S PRINCE WILLIAM AND KATE!

www.madamandeve.co.za

THAT'S **GREAT NEWS...DOES** MY MOTHER KNOW?

©RAPID PHASE · 2013

OH, SHE **KNOWS...**

... AND WE CONTINUE WITH **MORE** LIVE COVERAGE OF THE ROYAL BABY...

YAY!!

MADAM--I'M A LITTLE WORRIED ABOUT YOUR MOTHER. EVER SINCE THE "BIRTH" SHE SEEMS **OBSESSED** WITH THE **ROYAL FAMILY** AND ANYTHING **ENGLISH!**

SHE'S RIGHT! I'VE BEEN SITTING ON MY **KHYBER PASS**, WATCHING THE **CUSTARD AND JELLY** WITH A STIFF **GREGORY PECK!**

I'LL BE AT THE **RUB A DUB DUB** IF YOU WANT TO GIVE ME A TINKLE ON THE OL' **DOG AND BONE.**

www.madamandeve.co.za

SLAM!!

BRITISH RHYMING SLANG?!

I'M CALLING MY THERAPIST!

©RAPID PHASE · 2013

HERE YOU GO, MADAM. MY **WAGE INCREASE** DEMAND.

...AND HERE, **MY** OPENING OFFER.

HAHAHA!! HOHOHO!! HEE HEE HEE!

©RAPID PHASE · 2013

THE START OF THE **ANNUAL** WAGE NEGOTIATIONS. A GREAT TRADITION.

HAHAHA!!

HOHOHO!!

www.madamandeve.co.za

HELP THE **ECONOMIC FREEDOM FIGHTERS** FUND THEIR 2014 ELECTION CAMPAIGN BY BUYING FROM THIS NEW RANGE OF **EFF-**APPROVED MERCHANDISE AND SERVICES!

ECONOMIC FREEDOM LIGHTERS

EFF

ECONOMIC FREEDOM CIDERS

EFF

ECONOMIC FREEDOM ACTION FIGURES

Bzzt ... BLOODY AGENT!

EFF

ECONOMIC FREEDOM ACCOUNTANTS.

EFA

EFA

www.madamandeve.co.za © RAPID PHASE - 2013

ZZZZZZ...
HUH?

AAAAH!!

ALRIGHT! **WHOEVER** PUT THIS RED BERET ON MY **HEAD,** IS IN BIG TROUBLE!

GIGGLE!

MADAM & Eve

BY STEPHEN FRANCIS & RICO

AND IN OTHER NEWS, JULIUS MALEMA HAS SAID THE NAME OF HIS NEW PARTY, "THE ECONOMIC FREEDOM FIGHTERS"... WAS A CAREFULLY THOUGHT-OUT PROCESS.

RIGHT. LET'S VOTE... ALL IN FAVOUR OF "THE CORRUPTION-BUSTING BACKSTREET BERET BOYS," RAISE YOUR HAND.

THE "INDIAN-AFRIKANER SECRET ANTI-CONSPIRACY PARTY?"

TOO CONTROVERSIAL.

THE "WE WON'T KILL FOR ZUMA PARTY?!"

YOU MUST BE JOKING.

THE "AFRICANIST NATIONALISATION CONGRESS?"

"A...N...C?" ...EISH.

IDIOT.

MORON.

WAIT... WE NEED A NAME THE PEOPLE WILL REMEMBER! A TITLE OR NAME LIKE -- "LONG WALK TO FREEDOM!"

YES!   GO ON!

WE BELIEVE IN FREEDOM, RIGHT? ...AND WE'RE FIGHTERS... FIGHTERS FOR A FAIR ECONOMY!

THAT'S IT!!

"THE LONG WALK TO FIGHTING AND FREEDOM FROM ACCOUNTANTS PARTY!!"

KEEP THINKING... WE'RE CLOSE.

PRETTY GOOD.   NOT BAD, HUH?   I LIKE IT.

MIELLIES!!

HAPPY WOMEN'S DAY!!

YOU **BOUGHT** THE **WHOLE BAG**? YOU DON'T EVEN **LIKE** MIELIES!

SHUT UP AND HELP ME CARRY THESE TO THE KITCHEN.

FAMOUS WOMEN IN HISTORY

THE IRON LADY

JOAN OF THE DARK

G#X#@ ESKOM.

MADAM CURRY

MY TEACHER WANTS A WORD WITH YOU ABOUT **NOT** HELPING ME WITH MY **HOMEWORK ASSIGNMENTS** FROM NOW ON.

THE CROWD IS HUSHED AS THANDI **"TIGER"** SISULU IS GOING FOR HER 80th CAREER TITLE...

SHE'S **ONE STROKE** AWAY! IF SHE CAN **BIRDIE** THIS HOLE, THEN THE **CHAMPIONSHIP** IS HERS...

WHACK!

BONK!

WHO HIT ME WITH A G#X#@ **KIWI FRUIT?!**

MAYBE YOU SHOULD'VE USED A FIVE IRON.

JUST KEEP RUNNING!

MADAM & Eve

BY STEPHEN FRANCIS & RICO

THANDI.

NO, I **DON'T** HAVE IT. AND I'LL TELL YOU WHY:

LET ME TAKE YOU BACK... TO A COLD AUGUST MORNING... **56 YEARS AGO...**

TWENTY THOUSAND WOMEN STAGED A MARCH ON THE **UNION BUILDINGS** IN PRETORIA...

THEY CAME TO PROTEST THE **URBAN AREAS ACT,** COMMONLY KNOWN AS THE "PASS LAWS."

THEY LEFT PETITIONS OF **100 000** SIGNATURES... AND STOOD SOLEMNLY IN SILENCE FOR THIRTY MINUTES... MANY WITH THEIR CHILDREN ON THEIR BACKS.

SO HOW COULD I EVEN **THINK** OF **HOMEWORK** AT A TIME LIKE THIS?!

EXCELLENT! A NOVEL APPROACH! YOU GOT AN **A+!**

CLAP! CLAP! CLAP!

I DID?

THE ASSIGNMENT WAS AN ORAL REPORT ON A HISTORICAL EVENT!

©RAPID PHASE - 2013

YOU MEAN... I **LEARNED** SOMETHING IMPORTANT... BY **MISTAKE?!**

HAPPY WOMEN'S DAY.

It was ten minutes after breaking in, that one of the burglars realised that they may have picked the wrong house.

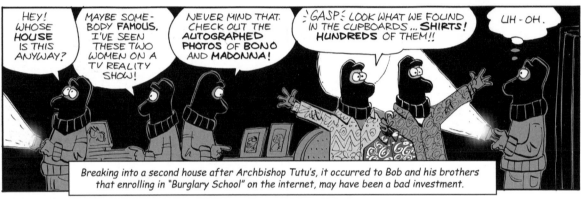

Breaking into a second house after Archbishop Tutu's, it occurred to Bob and his brothers that enrolling in "Burglary School" on the internet, may have been a bad investment.

MADAM & EVE

BY STEPHEN FRANCIS & RICO

THE SOUTH AFRICAN POLITICAL TAROT

DEAL OF ARMS

KING OF POTHOLES

THE KNIFE IN THE BACK

THE FOOL

THE TOWER

THE LEAKY CHARIOTS

THE MINER

THE MORAL HIGH GROUND

WELL... DO THE **TAROT CARDS** SAY I'LL BE RE-ELECTED AT **MANGAUNG** OR NOT?

DIFFICULT TO SAY, MISTER PRESIDENT...

...BUT YOU'RE DEFINITELY GETTING **MARRIED** AGAIN NEXT MONTH.

CRASH!!

L...A...Z...Y... "LAZY." THAT'S 16 POINTS.

WHAT ARE YOU PLAYING? SCRABBLE?

YEP.

HEY-LOOK AT THIS! "STINGY." DOUBLE WORD SCORE!

...AND IF I DIDN'T KNOW BETTER, I'D SWEAR SHE'S TRYING TO "TELL" ME SOMETHING WITH HER CHOICE OF WORDS.

OH, MADAM! DON'T BE RIDICULOUS!

www.madamandeve.co.za

©RAPID PHASE-2013

SIGH YOUR TURN.

IS "CHEAPSKATE" ONE WORD OR TWO?

August 1st, 20133333 33333333333333333 33333333333|

RATTLE! RATTLE! RATTLE!

©RAPID PHASE-2013

www.madamandeve.co.za

YOU SAID YOU DIDN'T MIND IF WE LEFT COOKIES WHILE WEB BROWSING.

SLAM!!

I.T. COMMUNICATION FAILURE.

MADAM & EVE'S

NEW TV REALITY SHOWS!

COMING SOON TO A BROADCASTER NEAR YOU!

THE AMAZING TAXI RACE

VROOOM!

SCREECH!

RUN FOR YOUR LIVES!

©RAPID PHASE-2013

The Horsemeat WHISPERER

PIES

PSST. CHICKEN & MUSHROOM? FILLED WITH GOAT'S MEAT, MORE LIKELY.

BRIBING BIG BROTHER

HELP ME OUT, BB... AND I'LL SPLIT THE MILLION BUCKS. YOU KNOW WHAT - I'M SAYING?

MADAM & Eve

BY STEPHEN FRANCIS & RICO

LOOK WHO JUST WALKED IN... ZWELINZIMA VAVI, WHO COSATU JUST SUSPENDED PENDING AN INVESTIGATION.

WHY DID HE CHOOSE OUR NEIGHBOURHOOD PUB?

The Indefinite Leave Bar & Grill

MAYBE HE LIKES THE PEANUTS.

OPEN

WELCOME TO THE NEIGHBOUR-HOOD, MISTER VAVI. I MAY NOT AGREE WITH YOUR POLITICS... AND ALTHOUGH YOU ADMITTED HAVING THAT AFFAIR WITH THE COSATU JUNIOR STAFFER...

...YEAH. RIGHT IN THE COSATU OFFICES.

AHEM.

...I STILL BELIEVE IN "DUE PROCESS" AND "INNOCENT UNTIL PROVEN GUILTY"... NOT SOME "SMEAR CAMPAIGN" OR TRIAL BY MEDIA.

THANK YOU...UH...

EDITH.

THANK YOU, EDITH.

COME HERE OFTEN? I BET YOU'RE A TAURUS. AM I RIGHT?

WAIT! COME BACK!! WHY DON'T YOU COME OVER TO MY PLACE FOR A LITTLE COLLECTIVE BARGAINING... INVITE YOUR FRIEND AND WE CAN FORM A TRI-PARTITE ALLIANCE.

©RAPID PHASE - 2013

HI, MOM. HOW WAS YOUR NIGHT OUT?

TIRING. A HIGH-PROFILE COSATU LEADER TRIED TO SCORE, BUT I SHOT HIM DOWN.

MOM. WHAT AN IMAGINATION.

MADAM & Eve

BY STEPHEN FRANCIS & RICO

Introducing
THE MADAM & EVE BOOK CLUB!

THIS WEEK IS AUTOBIOGRAPHY MONTH!

Join now -- and choose from these incredible page-turning South African autobiographies written by the men and women who lived them!

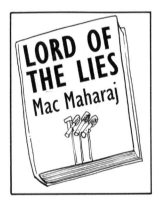

LORD OF THE LIES
Mac Maharaj

One Flew Over the Wedding Guests
The Gupta Brothers

The Great FATSBY
Kulubuse Zuma

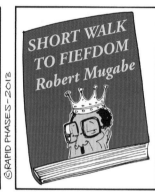

SHORT WALK TO FIEFDOM
Robert Mugabe

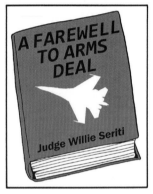

A FAREWELL TO ARMS DEAL
Judge Willie Seriti

©RAPID PHASES-2013

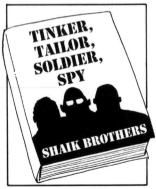

TINKER, TAILOR, SOLDIER, SPY
SHAIK BROTHERS

TENDER IS MY RIGHT
Julius Malema

NAKED LUNCH
Kenny Kunene

DRUNK MAN WALKING
TONY YENGENI

CRIME AND NO PUNISHMENT
JACOB ZUMA